THE APPLAUSE SCREENPLAY SERIES
Mark Mixson, General Editor

ERIK THE VIKING
THE SCREENPLAY

Written and directed by Terry Jones

*Including the
complete credits
with
Over 50 stills
from the movie*

THEATRE BOOK PUBLISHERS
New York • London

An Applause Original
ERIK THE VIKING
The Screenplay

Copyright © Orion Pictures and Erik the Viking Film Productions

Library of Congress Cataloging-in-Publication Data:
Jones, Terry, 1942-
    Erik the Viking: the screenplay / written and directed by Terry
Jones.
        p.   cm.   — (The Applause screenplay series)
    "Including the complete credits and an appendix of deleted scenes
with over 50 stills from the movie."
    ISBN 1-55783-054-1: $7.95
    I. Title.   II. Series.
PN1997.E687   1989
791.43'72—dc20
                                                                89-18034
                                                                CIP

Still Photography by David Appleby

APPLAUSE THEATRE BOOK PUBLISHERS
211 West 71st Street
New York, NY 10023
Phone 212-595-4735

ERIK THE VIKING
THE SCREENPLAY

1   **EXT.   VILLAGE   NIGHT**

Blackness.

Flames begin to lick upwards from the bottom of the
screen.

Suddenly all hell breaks loose. Screaming, yelling.
Black FIGURES flash across the foreground, with the
flames still burning behind.

Handheld, confused shots—burning, raping, killing and
looting—all very tight so we don't clearly see what's
going on.

2   **INT.   HELGA'S HUT   NIGHT**

The interior of a hut. The door is in the process of
being broken down. The CAMERA PANS slowly onto the
CLOSE-UP face of an attractive GIRL who is staring in
horrified fascination at the door. Her arms are white
with fresh dough and flour.

Suddenly the door bursts open and a wild-looking
VIKING leaps into the hut. He holds a sword. He looks
around wildly and then his eyes come to rest on the
GIRL.

This VIKING, I'm afraid, is ERIK. We are about to see
him in the worst possible light, so be prepared.

The GIRL cowers and looks terrified but resolute.

ERIK glances round.

Then slowly he advances on the GIRL. The GIRL reaches
behind her with her left hand and picks up a knife and
flings it with all her might at ERIK. He ducks,
however, and the knife embeds itself in the doorpost.
ERIK turns to look at it, then turns back and smiles.

Whereupon ERIK leaps on the GIRL, whose name is HELGA.

ERIK holds his sword to HELGA's throat with his right
hand, while his left hand searches to find the thongs
holding up his trousers.

(CONTINUED)

He is clearly having difficulty trying to hold his
heavy sword to HELGA's throat at the same time as
undoing his trousers. He fumbles and lowers his sword
for a moment and then recovers himself.

>   HELGA
> Have you done this sort of thing
> before?

>   ERIK
> Me? Of course! I've been looting and
> pillaging up and down the coast.

>   HELGA
>   (looking skeptical)
> Looting and pillaging, eh?

>   ERIK
>   (on the defensive)
> Yes.

>   HELGA
> What about the raping?

>   ERIK
> Shut up.

>   HELGA
> It's obvious you haven't raped anyone
> in your life.

>   ERIK
> Sh!

He covers her mouth with his free hand, and looks
around to make sure no one's heard. Then he carries on
trying to undo his trousers, but he is now somewhat
less than half-hearted about it.

HELGA watches suspiciously.

>   HELGA
> Do you *like* women?

ERIK is clearly shocked and stung by the insinuation.
He stops.

>   ERIK
>   (indignantly)
> Of course I like women ... I *love* 'em.

>   (CONTINUED)

> HELGA
> (pointing out the
> obvious)
> You don't love *me*.

> ERIK
> (as if remembering
> himself)
> No ... right ... this is *rape* ...
> Mark you, I'm not saying I couldn't
> get to like you ... in fact ... well,
> to be quite honest I prefer it when
> there's some sort of mutual feeling
> between two people ...

> HELGA
> What - rape?

> ERIK
> No. It isn't rape then is it?

> HELGA
> Oh, get it over with.

> ERIK
> (hesitates again)
> I don't suppose ... no ...

> HELGA
> What?

> ERIK
> I don't suppose you ... you *do* like
> me at all?

> HELGA
> What d'you expect? You come in here,
> burn my village, kill my family and
> try to rape me ...

This is too much for ERIK. He withers under the irony,
and gives up. And walks over to the other side of the
room.

> ERIK
> I'll kill you if you say anything
> about this to anyone.

(CONTINUED)

                         HELGA
                        (puzzled)
              About raping me?

                         ERIK
              About *not* raping you ...

                         HELGA
              You *don't* like it, do you?

                         ERIK
              Well, it just seems a bit crude,
              that's all.

                         HELGA
              What about the killing and looting?
              That's just as crude, isn't it?

                         ERIK
              Oh, well, you've *got* to do them.

                         HELGA
              Why? Why have you got to go 'round
              killing and looting?

                         ERIK
              To pay for the next expedition, of
              course.

                         HELGA
              But that's a circular argument! If
              the only reason for going on an
              expedition is the killing and looting
              and the only reason for the killing
              and looting is to pay for the next
              expedition, they cancel each other
              out.

                         ERIK
              Oh! Stop talking as if we were
              married!

                         HELGA
              Well, you started it.

                         ERIK
              I just said I didn't feel like raping
              you.

                                        (CONTINUED)

                              HELGA
              And *I* was just saying that rape is no
              more pointless or crude than all the
              killing and looting that goes on.

ERIK vents some of his frustration on the already
shattered door.

                              ERIK
              Scream.

                              HELGA
              Ah.

                              ERIK
              Louder.

                              HELGA
              Aaaagh! Rape!

                              ERIK
                      (he'd forgotten
                      about that)
              Oh, thanks.

Suddenly the door bursts open on the catch and two
more VIKINGS leap in with eager eyes blazing. They
have the very unfortunate names of EARNEST and
JENNIFER, but it doesn't really matter for reasons
which will become obvious very quickly. They are also
slightly drunk.

                              EARNEST
                      (eagerly)
              Rape?

                              JENNIFER
                      (looking around)
              Where?

JENNIFER-THE-VIKING sways and leans against a door
post. The MARAUDERS' eyes come to rest on ERIK and
HELGA who are standing, fully clothed, about six feet
apart. They look slightly puzzled.

                              HELGA
              He raped me standing up.

There is a pause. ERIK looks at HELGA. Why has she
saved his face by telling this lie?

                                        (CONTINUED)

> JENNIFER
> (to ERIK)
> You finished, then?

> ERIK
> Oh ... yes ... I suppose so ...

> EARNEST
> Right! Me first!

> JENNIFER
> No! I asked!

EARNEST leaps on top of HELGA and pins her to the ground. JENNIFER joins in.

ERIK looks stunned for a moment. Then he suddenly leaps to HELGA's defence.

> ERIK
> Leave her alone!

He pulls JENNIFER off, but JENNIFER fights back. ERIK forces JENIFER back until she falls into the kneading trough. They fight in the dough for some moments, until ERIK runs JENNIFER through. The dough is stained red, and the film is rid of such an inappropriately named Viking once and for all.

ERIK then turns his attention to EARNEST who is still on top of HELGA. Without a moment's hesitation, ERIK runs him through the back. EARNEST sreams. So does HELGA. ERIK turns white, and pulls out his sword.

EARNEST falls over into a heap with his co-misnomer, and ERIK kneels beside HELGA to find a blood stain under her breast where he has inadvertently run her through. She is clearly not long for this world.

> HELGA
> Thanks for saving me from a fate
> worse than death.

> ERIK
> I didn't mean to!

> HELGA
> (gasping for breath)
> Oh, that's all right then ... it's
> the thought ... that counts ...

(CONTINUED)

                          ERIK
          You told them I raped you – why?

                          HELGA
                          (dying)
          I dunno ... you looked so ... so
          vulnerable ...

                          ERIK
          Why should you care?

                          HELGA
                          (dying)
          Why ... should *you* care?

                          ERIK
          Tell me your name?

HELGA looks up at him, but dies in his arms, without
ever saying her name.

                          ERIK
          Tell me ... what *is* it? ...

ERIK realizes that she has gone. He gazes at her for
some time. A tear comes to his eye. He looks around at
the two dead bodies beside them. Then he listens to
the sounds of raping and slaughter continuing on the
outside. Screams and bloodthirsty shouts echo
alongside the roar of flames and the cries of animals.
The CAMERA tracks in to a big CLOSE-UP on ERIK.
SUPERIMPOSE the TITLE: ERIK THE VIKING:

SECOND TITLE: TIM ROBBINS

MIX THROUGH TO WIDE SHOT of the burning village.
FIGURES are running here and there.

SUPERIMPOSE THE REST OF THE OPENING TITLES.

By the last of the titles the last of the flames are
dying down.

3   INT.   MEAD HALL IN ERIK'S HOME TOWN OF RAVENSFJORD
     NIGHT

CLOSE ON a very tough looking VIKING, THORFINN
SKULL-SPLITTER, rushing up to CAMERA. He screams and
hurls an axe.

                                        (CONTINUED)

CUT TO:

A CLOSE-UP of the axe thudding into the wall. PAN across to the frightened face of a girl, UNN, who is pinned to the wall with her braids spread out. The VIKINGS are hurling axes at her à la Kirk Douglas in *The Vikings*.

CUT TO:

SVEN's DAD, LOKI and SNORRI laughing rather unpleasantly.

CUT TO:

ERIK, frowning. He is sitting on a dais at a table reserved for his GRANDAD, who is clearly the chief of the little village, and his MUM who sits on the other side of his GRANDAD.

His GRANDAD is guffawing unpleasantly. His MUM frowns slightly.

ANGLE ON THORKATLA dipping a large jug into one of the vats of ale. She looks suddenly fearful and moves away quickly. We PAN onto the group of VIKINGS who are doing the axe-throwing, and we see the reason for her sudden fear: the drunk THORFINN has just pressed an axe into the hand of the practically legless IVAR THE BONELESS, and the others are now pushing IVAR up to the throwing position. It's a bit like darts. IVAR is clearly in no condition to throw anything accurately except perhaps the contents of his stomach.

ANGLE ON one of the WOMEN, THORHILD, looking anxious, as she pauses in her ministrations of ale from a large jug.

CUT TO:

UNN looking desperate.

ANGLE ON IVAR. Amidst much giggling and drunken hysterics, he throws wildly.

CUT TO:

THORHILD. Her jug smashes as the axe travels through it on its way to a destination that is certainly not UNN.

(CONTINUED)

PAN along the ale-bench. Many of the VIKINGS sitting
at it are considerably amused by this incident. A few
of them, however, have reached the maudlin stage and
haven't got the energy to laugh at anything, beyond a
sarcastic grunt. SNORRI is one of these.

ANGLE ON IVAR's MUM and THORFINN's MUM both frowning.

ANGLE ON ERIK frowning. His GRANDAD digs him in the
ribs, almost helpless with merriment.

                                           CUT TO:

ERIK'S POINT-OF-VIEW of UNN. A heap of axes lies at
her feet, and many others are bristling out of the
wall behind her.

ANGLE ON the group of DRUNKEN AXE THROWERS. It is now
SVEN's turn. He is well and truly plastered. IVAR has
probably collapsed on the floor helplessly giggling.

UNN cringes.

SVEN throws the axe with total abandon and without
stopping to take aim. UNN flinches and shuts her eyes,
prepared for the worst. Then she hears a whoop of
mirth and realizes she's all right still. She opens
her eyes and looks to her left.

ANGLE ON an extremely drunk VIKING who is sitting at
the cooking table with his back to us. SVEN's axe is
imbedded in his back. He doesn't seem to have noticed,
but slowly slumps forward on to the table. The CAMERA
refocuses on HARALD MISSIONARY who is sitting
opposite. Behind him hovers an anxious GRIMHILD
HOUSEWIFE.

HARALD thinks for a moment that he ought to do
something, but then realizes that it's too late, and
simply takes another swig of ale.

SVEN and the OTHERS are beside themselves.

LOKI and CO. on the ale-bench think it's pretty funny,
too. Even SNORRI can't help a smirk.

CLOSE-UP of ERIK frowning.

THORFINN is now pressing a second axe into the
blind-drunk SVEN's hands. EVERYONE goes quiet. The

                                      (CONTINUED)

WOMEN look deadfully anxious.

LOKI and CO. look a bit apprehensive but still amused.

HARALD cringes

UNN cringes.

SVEN laughs wildly and throws.

HARALD ducks as the axe thuds into the wall behind his
head.

UNN shuts her eyes in relief.

At this juncture the VIKINGS have run out of axes.
THORFINN SKULL-SPLITTER holds up his hand.

> THORFINN
> (drunkenly)
> Hold it!

He nods and several rush forward to pick up the mass
of axes. At the same time, HARALD GREYCLOAK hurries up
to UNN, holding his dog-eared Bible.

> HARALD GREYCLOAK
> If you were thinking of converting,
> my dear, this would be an *ideal*
> opportunity ...

> UNN
> Not now!

> HARALD GREYCLOAK
> No, of course not –
> > (he turns to go away
> > and then hesitates)
> You might *not* get another chance, you
> know ...

> UNN
> Go away.

> HARALD GREYCLOAK
> ... Yes, of course.

At this moment an axe thuds into the wall behind UNN.
The MONK takes a fearful look back, sees the VIKINGS
have recovered their axes.

(CONTINUED)

>   HARALD GREYCLOAK
>   (crossing himself)
>   I'll pray for you anyway, dear ...
>   Yes ... That's what I'll do ...

A large earthenware pot is suddenly shattered, and
HARALD scurries off to the mead-bench. The
axe-throwing continues with renewed vigor but no
greater accuracy.

On the dais sits ERIK's GRANDDAD, the old chieftain,
looking on and enjoying the fun.

Meanwhile the poor GIRL at whose braids the axes are
being thrown is quite distraught. ERIK looks at her
and, for a moment, sees HELGA in her place.

Finally IVAR's MUM, who is serving, has had enough.
She bangs down the jugs of ale she is carrying and
rounds on the MEN.

>   IVAR's MUM
>   Let her go!

>   THORFINN
>   Why?

>   VIKINGS
>   Yes, why?

>   SVEN THE STRONG
>   Why should we let her go?

>   THORFINN
>   We haven't hit a single braid yet!

The VIKINGS all guffaw.

IVAR's MUM has had enough. She throws the contents of
two jugs of ale over THORFINN. He is soaked, but after
the first shock he grins evilly, because now he's been
given carte blanche to do the thing he enjoys doing
most. Without another thought he throws a vicious
right hook at IVAR's MUM and lays her out cold.

>   CUT TO:

ERIK reacting with disgust.

>   (CONTINUED)

3   CONTINUED:

His GRANDAD, however, gives a whoop of glee.

> GRANDAD
> Whoah! Heee! That showed her!

Meanwhile a little shrivelled OLD MAN is jumping up
and down.

> INGEMUND THE OLD
> Hey! He hit my wife!

INGEMUND starts to go for THORFINN, but THORHILD beats
him to it. She grabs one of the long-handled cooking
griddles from the fires and swings it at THORFINN.

THORFINN, however, ducks, and the red-hot griddle hits
SVEN THE STRONG, who is standing with his back to
THORFINN.

SVEN screams and goes berserk, turning around and
hitting THORFINN who is now standing upright again.

> INGEMUND THE OLD
> Leave him alone!

INGEMUND hits SVEN. THORFINN hits INGEMUND, and a
general fight breaks out.

The WOMEN join in, tables are overturned, and PEOPLE
fall on the fire and so on and so forth.

ANGLE ON ERIK's GRANDAD. He is thoroughly enjoying it
all, but ERIK looks at it in disgust and at his
GRANDAD in despair. Eventually ERIK gets up and walks
out of the Mead Hall.

His GRANDAD notices and frowns. He knows something's
wrong with his grandson but hasn't a clue what it
could be. ERIK's MOTHER frowns and nods to his
GRANDAD.

GRANDAD gets up and fights his way through the melee
to follow ERIK out of the Hall.

4   EXT.   THE SEASHORE AT RAVENSFJORD   DAY

ANGLE ON the sea, pounding on the rocks. The sky is
black and boiling.

(CONTINUED)

ERIK is walking broodingly along the margin of the water. His GRANDAD catches up with him. In the distance we hear the sounds of the fight in the Mead Hall.

>   GRANDAD
>   What's the matter, son?

ERIK doesn't reply. His eyes go back to the Mead Hall. His GRANDAD follows his glance.

>   GRANDAD
>   We're missing all the fun ...

>   ERIK
>   What's it all about?

>   GRANDDAD
>   What?

>   ERIK
>   We toil and labor, we loot and
>   pillage, rape and kill ... and yet ...

>   GRANDDAD
>   You talking piffle, son.

>   ERIK
>   Where does it all get us, Grandpa?

>   GRANDDAD
>   Who have you been talking to?

>   ERIK
>   I met this girl ...

>   GRANDDAD
>   It's always the women that start the
>   trouble.

>   ERIK
>   She got me thinking ...

>   GRANDDAD
>   So? What'd you do to her?

ERIK stops in his tracks-as if brought up short by the horror of what he has done.

(CONTINUED)

> ERIK
> I ... I ... *killed* her ...

> GRANDDAD
> That's my boy!

ERIK'S GRANDDAD gives him a paternal hug. ERIK looks at him and thinks about the generation gap.

5   **EXT.   A LANDSCAPE OF SNOW AND ICE   DAY**

ANGLE ON feet running through the snow. Only the sound of ERIK. We hear his voice:

> ERIK (V.O.)
> Freya?

> CUT TO:

ERIK's face as he runs. He looks around him and calls out again.

6   **EXT.   FREYA'S CAVE   DAY**

A REMOTE, BARREN MOUNTAINSIDE.

ERIK climbs INTO SHOT, and continues climbing until he reaches a cave. As his eyes get used to the dark, he can make out a few signs of life: a cooking pot on a fire, a straw bed, a pile of rune-sticks.

> ERIK
> Freya! Freya!

There is a bundle of rags behind ERIK. A HEAD rises from it. This is FREYA.

> FREYA
> Ah ... Erik ... Erik the "Viking" ...

It is not clear whether her words are not a little mocking. She indicates for him to sit by the fire. They sit. Silence. FREYA looks at ERIK, who seems intent on peering into the fire.

> FREYA
> Now what *can* you want with me, Erik the "Viking"?

(CONTINUED)

Again there is a hint of mockery in her voice. ERIK
doesn't reply.

He looks at FREYA and then throws a stone into the
fire.

> ERIK
> I shouldn't have come.

> FREYA
> They will make fun of you for
> listening to an old woman's stories?

ERIK doesn't reply. FREYA watches him craftily.

> FREYA
> Young men are only interested in
> fighting and killing.

ERIK looks up at her sharply. It is as if she has read
his mind. Then he goes back to studying the fire, as
if looking for an answer there.

> ERIK
> But has it always been like that,
> Freya? From the beginning of time?

FREYA doesn't reply for a bit. Then she takes ERIK's
hand and leads him to the mouth of the cave. They look
out at the grey, desolate landscape: nothing but
arctic wastes, snow and desolation. Above them the
black clouds boil ceaselessly; it could be twilight.

> FREYA
> What do you see, Erik?

> ERIK
> I see the world.

> FREYA
> Is it night or day, Erik?

> ERIK
> It is day, of course, Freya.

> FREYA
> Is it summer or winter, Erik?

ERIK looks around at the snowy wastes and then looks
back at FREYA, puzzled.

(CONTINUED)

                              ERIK
                    The winter is passed, thank goodness,
                    Freya. It is summer.

FREYA puts her face close to ERIK's and peers into his
eyes.

                              FREYA
                    Have you ever seen the sun, Erik?

                              ERIK
                    The sun is up beyond the clouds-
                    where it always is.

                              FREYA
                    But have you ever seen it? Think
                    back ...

                              ERIK
                    Of course not ... but ... when I was a
                    child ... I remember a dream ... it
                    was as if the whole sky were blue ...

                              FREYA
                    The sky *was* blue, Erik ... once ...

ERIK looks at her.

                              FREYA
                    The Old Stories tell of an age that
                    would come such as this - when Fenrir
                    the Wolf would swallow the sun, and a
                    Great Winter would settle upon the
                    world. It was to be an axe age, a
                    sword age, a storm age, when brother
                    would turn against brother and men
                    would fight each other until the
                    world would finally be destroyed.

ERIK looks out across the bleak and gloomy landscape
and the black boiling clouds in the sky.

                              ERIK
                         (almost to himself)
                    Then ... this is the Age of Ragnarok?

FREYA turns to go back into the cave. ERIK runs after
her.

                                              (CONTINUED)

> ERIK
> Wait, Freya!

FREYA turns.

> ERIK
> Is there nothing men can do?

> FREYA
> The Gods are asleep, Erik.

FREYA turns, and ERIK lets her go. Then he runs after
her again.

> ERIK
> I will go and wake them up!

FREYA turns and looks at him. She clearly enjoys his
earnest enthusiasm, but is afraid he doesn't know what
he is talking about.

> ERIK
> Tell me what I must do, Freya!

FREYA thinks for some moments. Then she turns and sits
back by her fire. ERIK watches her, waiting.

> FREYA
> Erik ... far out in the midst of the
> Western Ocean there is a land ... men
> call it Hy-Brasil. There you will
> find a horn that is called
> Resounding. You must take the Horn
> Resounding, and three times you must
> blow it. The first note will take you
> to Asgaard. The second will awaken
> the Gods, and the third note will
> bring you home. But remember ... once
> you are in the spell of the Horn,
> hatred will destroy you.

ERIK turns to go and then hesitates:

> ERIK
> And will the dead ever return, Freya?

> FREYA
> That I cannot tell you.

7   EXT.   RAVENSFJORD   DAY

THORFINN SKULL-SPLITTER is having his head banged on
the ground by an enraged SVEN THE STRONG.

Suddenly ERIK pushes his way through the crowd,
marches up to the TWO PROTAGONISTS and separates them.

There is general disgruntlement all around at this,
and murmurs of: "Who does he think he is?"

                    ERIK'S GRANDAD
          What are you doing, Erik? Thorfinn
          just said Sven's Grandfather died of
          old age.

                    INGEMUND THE OLD
          They must fight to the death.

                    THORFINN
          That's right! Sven must kill me.

                    OTHERS
          Yes. You stay out of this. What's it
          to do with you?
                    (etc.)

SVEN grinds his teeth and struggles to get at
THORFINN, but ERIK still keeps them apart.

                    ERIK
          Aren't you afraid of death, Thorfinn
          Skull-Splitter?

THORFINN shrugs.

                    THORFINN
          Not death by the sword! It means I
          shall drink in Valhalla, with the
          great warriors.

                                        CUT TO:

HARALD THE MISSIONARY engaging THORHILD.

                    HARALD THE MISSIONARY
          You don't believe in all that
          Valhalla stuff, do you?

                                        (CONTINUED)

                    18

                         THORHILD
          Go away.

                         HARALD
          Fine ... right ... just checking.

He moves off.

                         ERIK
          And you, Sven, aren't you afraid of
          crossing the Rainbow Bridge to
          Asgaard?

                         SVEN
          I will join my grandfather there.

                         THORFINN
          He's not in Valhalla! He died of old
          age!

                         SVEN
          You liar!

They start trying to kill each other again, and crash
through a fence into a pig-sty. PIGS squeal and run in
all directions.

ERIK wades into the pen and separates them again.

                         ERIK
          Stop it!

                         OTHERS
          Leave them alone! Keep out of it,
          Erik!

The OTHERS pull ERIK away.

                         GRANDAD
          There's only one way to settle it.

                         EVERYONE
          Yes!

                         THORFINN
          He *must* kill me!

                         EVERYONE
          Yes! That's right!
                    (etc.)

                                   (CONTINUED)

SVEN struggles to oblige. ERIK dives back to keep them apart.

> ERIK
> There is another way.

> GRANDAD
> Who gets killed?

> ERIK
> Nobody gets killed.

> THORFINN
> Oh well ...

He starts attacking SVEN again. ERIK once again pulls them apart.

> ERIK
> But it will be dangerous. Maybe none of us will return.

> SNORRI
> Ah well, that's much more sensible than just Thorfinn getting killed. Shall we all go and pack now?

> SVEN
> What are you talking about, Erik?

> ERIK
> What if we could find Bi-Frost the Rainbow Bridge?

This causes a sensation amongst everyone watching, on the lines of "You can't do that" and so on. They scoff at ERIK.

> THORFINN
> (in disbelief)
> *Find* the Rainbow Bridge?

> ERIK

> Find it ... *and* cross it!

Super sensation amongst everyone — except for HARALD THE MISSIONARY who shakes his head sadly and looks up to heaven.

(CONTINUED)

> HARALD
> Look! You can't find somewhere that
> doesn't exist.

> GRANDAD
> (to Harald)
> Shut up!

HARALD shrugs.

> SVEN
> Only the dead reach Asgaard, Erik.

> ERIK
> What's the matter? Are you afraid to
> try?

THORFINN and SVEN are put on the defensive.

> THORFINN
> Of course we're not afraid to try,
> but ...

ERIK turns on THORFINN, sensing he has the advantage.

> ERIK
> 'But' what?

> THORFINN
> But ...

> ERIK
> What?

THORFINN and SVEN exchange glances. SVEN comes to his
rescue.

> SVEN
> Nobody's ever crossed the Rainbow
> Bridge to Asgaard.

> ERIK
> We'd be the first!

> SNORRI
> You mean we'd be dead?

> ERIK
> No! We'd be the first living men to
> set foot in the halls of the Gods.

(CONTINUED)

Pause. Uncomfortable shifting.

>   SVEN
>   But *how*?

>   ERIK
>   I don't know—but I'm not afraid to
>   try.

>   THORFINN
>   Well, I'm certainly not, either.

>   SVEN
>   Neither am I.

>   ERIK
>   Then you'll come.

>   HARALD
>   But there isn't such a place as ...
>   Look ...

>   THORFINN & SVEN
>   Shut up.

>   ERIK
>   What d'you say?

>   SVEN
>   Well ... I'm game.

>   THORFINN
>   Me, too.

ERIK grins. He has persuaded them against their will.

>   GRANDAD
>   Aren't you going to go on fighting?

>   SVEN & THORFINN
>   No.

>   GRANDAD
>   Oh ...

There is general disappointment all around.

>   IVAR THE BONELESS
>   Oh, go on ...

(CONTINUED)

> GRANDAD
> Just have a bit of a fight.

> INGEMUND THE OLD
> *I'll* fight someone.

> GRANDAD
> You're too old.

> INGEMUND THE OLD
> No, I ain't.

8   EXT.   THE QUAY   RAVENSFJORD   DAY

Under a heavy black sky a LONGSHIP is being repaired and fitted out for a journey. ERIK is there directing operatings. Provisions are being placed in the ship. CARPENTERS are replacing planks. The sails are spread out on the ground and being sewn up. Inspiring MUSIC.

9   EXT.   KEITEL BLACKSMITH'S FORGE   DAY

The CAMERA PANS around all the activity and comes to rest on KEITEL BLACKSMITH. He is a magnificent mountain of a man in an Arnold Schwarzeneggarish sort of way. He hammers a sword and sparks fly, but his eyes keep returning to the preparations for the voyage. Clearly something is worrying him.

His assitant, LOKI, sidles up to him.

> LOKI
> Wish you were going, too?

KEITEL grunts angrily and plunges the sword into cold water. Steam and bubbles.

> LOKI
> But you *can't* because you're too
> busy.

KEITEL pulls the sword out of the water and tests it. It slices like a razor. LOKI watches.

> LOKI
> Charge Hodur 15 for that one. It's a
> good one.

(CONTINUED)

> KEITEL
> Yes, it is good. But I told him 10.

> LOKI
> You can charge him what you like.

LOKI takes the sword from KEITEL and stacks it alongside a lot more freshly made swords.

> LOKI
> You just can't make enough swords and spears and knives and daggers to satisfy the demand. You could charge Hodur 20 and he'd pay it.

> KEITEL
> (shocked)
> Oh, I couldn't do that! The Blacksmith's Code says ...

> LOKI
> Yes, yes ... of course ... the "Blacksmith's Code" ...

KEITEL goes back to his forge and pulls out a fresh dollop of white-hot ore. LOKI comes up behind him.

> LOKI
> If this *is* the Age of Ragnarok, Keitel Blacksmith, it is *good* to us.

> KEITEL
> (banging with his hammer)
> Can't make enough swords!

BANG! BANG! BANG!

> KEITEL
> Can't make enough axe-heads!

BANG! BANG! BANG!

> LOKI
> But, Keitel, if Erik ever finds the Horn Resounding ... if he ever crosses Bi-Frost, the Rainbow Bridge ... if he ever wakens the Gods ...

KEITEL stops smiting the metal on his forge. He stares

(CONTINUED)

into space.

> KEITEL
> They chase Fenrir the Wolf from the
> sky ...

> LOKI
> The Age of Ragnarok ends ...

> KEITEL
> The bottom falls out of the sword
> business!

> LOKI
> It's not just *your* livelihood that's
> at stake, but your son's, and the
> livelihood of *all* blacksmiths.

> KEITEL
> (this touches a
> nerve in his
> muscular mind)
> My Brother Blacksmiths!

> LOKI
> That's right.

> KEITEL
> The Blacksmith's code says I must ...

> LOKI
> Honor and protect all blacksmiths.

> KEITEL
> (as if reciting a
> song or oath)
> Together we stand!

> LOKI
> You can't let Erik do *that*.

LOKI smiles. He has KEITEL playing into his hands
although KEITEL doesn't realize it.

FADE.

10 EXT.   THE QUAY   RAVENSFJORD   DAY

Some days later. The expedition is set to leave.

(CONTINUED)

THORFINN SKULL-SPLITTER taking leave of his MUM and
DAD.

> THORFINN'S MUM
> And you've got *both* axes?

> THORFINN
> Yes, Mother.

> THORFINN'S MUM
> And something to sharpen them with?

> THORFINN
> Yes, Mum.

> THORFINN'S MUM
> And don't forget: never let your
> enemy get behind you.

> THORFINN
> No, Mother.

> THORFINN'S MUM
> And keep your sword greased.

> THORFINN
> Yes, Mother. Goodbye, Dad.

> THORFINN'S DAD
> And don't forget to wash – you know –
> *all* over.

> THORFINN
> No, Dad.

> THORFINN'S MUM
> And if you have to kill somebody,
> *kill* them! Don't stop to think about
> it.

> THORFINN
> (mildly)
> I never do. ...

11   EXT.   SVEN'S HUT   DAY

SVEN THE STRONG who is also being lectured. The
lecture is coming from his FATHER – ULF THE
MADDENINGLY CALM.

(CONTINUED)

                        SVEN'S FATHER
                         (sotto voce)
             It's a tradition.

                            SVEN
             I know, Dad.

                        SVEN'S FATHER
             I was a berserk for King Harald
             Fairhair ...

                            SVEN
             You went berserk ...

                        SVEN'S FATHER
             I went berserk in every battle I ever
             fought for King Harald ...

                            SVEN
             So did your father ...

                        SVEN'S FATHER
             So did my father and his father
             before him.

                            SVEN
             But it's a responsibility ...

                        SVEN'S FATHER
             But it's a responsibility being a
             Berserk.

                            SVEN
             I must only let the red rage ...

                        SVEN'S FATHER
             You must only let the red rage take
             hold of you in the thick of battle.

                            SVEN
                         (losing his temper)
             I KNOW! I'VE HEARD IT ALL A THOUSAND
             TIMES!

They have reached the quay. A sudden silence falls, as
all the VILLAGE turns to stare nervously at SVEN.
SVEN'S FATHER shakes his head slowly.

                                            (CONTINUED)

                         SVEN'S FATHER
                No, no ... you'll never make a
                Berserk. If you let it out now, you'll
                have nothing left for battle ...

                         IVAR'S MUM
                Besides ... it's dangerous.

                         SVEN'S FATHER
                     (gloomily)
                It's the end of a family tradition.

12 EXT.   QUAYSIDE   RAVENSFJORD   DAY

LEIF THE LUCKY standing with his PREGNANT GIRLFRIEND.

                         GIRL
                Bye, Leif.

                         LEIF
                Bye ... sorry ...

                         GIRL
                Yeah ... well ...

                         LEIF
                You will wait?

                         GIRL
                What d'you expect me to do?

She hugs him – tears in their eyes. Then she takes a
bracelet off her arm and gives it to LEIF.

                         GIRL
                Wear this for luck.

LEIF looks at it.

                         LEIF
                That's what they call me ... Leif the
                Lucky.

                         GIRL
                Please.

LEIF takes it and puts it on.

13 EXT.   GOLDEN DRAGON   DAY

HARALD THE MISSIONARY dumping a bag on board the ship.
GRIMHILD HOUSEWIFE is helping him.

SNORRI looks at him in surprise.

                    SNORRI
          You coming? You don't even believe in
          Asgaard.

                    HARALD
          I thought I might do a bit of
          business on the way.

                    SNORRI
          You're wasting your time.

                    HARALD
          Listen. I've been in this dump for 16
          years and I haven't made a single
          convert ...

                    SNORRI
          There was Thorbjorn Vifilsson's wife.
          You converted *her*.

                    HARALD
          Thorbjorn Vifilsson's wife became a
          Buddhist, not a Christian.

                    SNORRI
          Same thing, isn't it?

                    HARALD
          No, it is *not*.

14 EXT. FAR END OF RAVENSFJORD AND COUNTRYSIDE   DAY

ANGLE ON LOKI as he straps a large consignment of
swords onto a pony and then mounts another and sneaks
surreptitiously out of the village, over the barren
hills of Iceland, under the boiling black skies of
Ragnarok.

15 EXT.   QUAYSIDE   RAVENSFJORD   DAY

ANGLE ON ERIK, standing on the quay in front of the

                                        (CONTINUED)
                    29

Golden Dragon. The longship is now loaded and ready to sail.

ERIK's GRANDAD is shaking ERIK by the hand in a parting ceremony. GRANDAD nods at the VILLAGERS and whispers to ERIK.

> GRANDAD
> I think you should say something.

> ERIK
> Oh ... yes ...

ERIK addresses the VILLAGE.

> ERIK
> Well ... we'll be off now ...

ERIK'S GRANDAD waits for some time before he realizes that ERIK doesn't intend to say anything else.

> GRANDAD
> You need to say a bit more than that!

> ERIK
> Oh ... er ... yes ...

The faces of the VILLAGE FOLK turn toward him. There are many moist eyes. ERIK'S MOTHER starts to cry. His GRANDDAD comforts her.

> ERIK
> Oh, there, Mum ...
>> (he turns and
>> addresses everyone)
> Don't be sad ... you all know why
> we're going, so don't grieve. Maybe
> untold dangers do lie ahead of us, and
> some of you may well be looking at the
> one you love for the last time ...

SOMEONE bursts out sobbing. ERIK desperately tries to rally their spirits.

> ERIK
> But don't grieve! Even though the
> Hordes of Muspel tear us limb from
> limb ... or the Fire Giants burn each
> and every one of us to a cinder ...
>> (more)

(CONTINUED)

                            ERIK (CONT.)
More crying.

              ... though we may be swallowed by the
              Dragon of the North Sea or fall off
              the Edge of the World ... don't cry.

More crying.

              No! *Don't* cry ...

By this time most of the VILLAGE is blubbering
profusely.

HARALD THE MISSIONARY slips his arm around his weeping
girl friend, GRIMHILD HOUSEWIFE.

                       HARALD THE MISSIONARY
              Sh ... There ... it's all fantasy,
              there's no Dragon of the North Sea,
              no Edge of the World ...

                            GRIMHILD
              That's what *you* say.

                            ERIK
                       (aside to his
                        Grandad)
              What's the matter with them?

                            GRANDAD
              Just say something cheerful.

                            ERIK
              Oh ... right!
                       (he can't think of
                        anything)
              Well ... *CHEERS*, everybody!

ERIK smiles broadly and waves. The entire VILLAGE
stares back at him with tears in their eyes, and
biting their lips. Suddenly ONE MOTHER can't hold it
back anymore.

                       THORFINN's MUM
              Don't go!

ANOTHER MOTHER rushes out and grabs IVAR THE BONELESS.

                                        (CONTINUED)

> IVAR's MUM
> My son! I don't want you to go!

> IVAR
> I don't want to go, either ...

> ERIK
> Oh, gods! Please, everybody! Keep
> calm! It's not certain *all* of us are
> going to die ... and in any case we
> may not die *hideous* deaths ...

More renewed sobbing. GRANDAD's eyes go heavenward.

> GRANDAD
> (to ERIK)
> I think we should go ...

> ERIK
> Right.
> (he turns for a last
> salute)
> Farewell ... for the last time ...
> may the gods prevent ...

> GRANDAD
> No, don't say anything else!

Suddenly KEITEL THE BLACKSMITH steps forward. His
muscles ripple. His handsome face radiates heroism and
manliness.

> KEITEL
> Wait, Erik!

> ERIK
> Keitel Blacksmith?

They stop and turn.

> KEITEL
> You can't go without me. Who will
> repair your swords and mend your
> shields?

Renewed sobs from the WOMEN.

> WOMEN
> Oh, no! Ah, lackaday! Not *him,* too!

(CONTINUED)

                         ERIK
           What's the matter *now*?

                         UNN
           If Keitel Blacksmith goes with you ...

                         THORHILD
           We'll have no one to do the things he
           did for us.

                         THORKATLA
           Or sharpen our knives and make our
           pans.

An awkward silence. The OTHERS all turn on her and
frown - a bit of shin-kicking goes on. It's clear that
KEITEL is popular amongst the WOMENFOLK. ERIK doesn't
notice.

                         ERIK
           You will have Keitel's assisstant
           Loki to do all that.

                         WOMEN
           Loki? Eurrgh!

                         ERIK
           What's wrong with Loki? He's becoming
           very good at blacksmithing.

                         WOMEN
           Yes ... but ...

                         THORKATLA
           He's so small and ...

The OTHERS shush her up. More shin-kicking.

                         THORHILD
                    (innocently)
           Oh, yes ... we've got Loki ... that's
           true ...

16 EXT.   **HALFDAN THE BLACK'S CASTLE**   DAY

ANGLE ON LOKI riding across a bleak landscape. He
approaches a GRIM CASTLE. Ravens fly overhead.
Contorted skeletons dangle from poles.

                                        (CONTINUED)

LOKI dismounts and hammers on the great wooden doors.
They open and a GRIM GUARD bars the way.

>   GUARD
>   What is your business?

>   LOKI
>   (a trifle nervous)
>   I wish to speak to Halfdan the Black.

>   GUARD
>   He's too busy.

>   LOKI
>   I have money! See!

He holds out a gold coin. The GUARD grabs it and nods
LOKI into the castle.

17 **EXT.   COURTYARD OF HALFDAN'S CASTLE   DAY**

Within the courtyard is a dismal sight. WRETCHED MEN
and WOMEN are being tortured. Some are tied up on
frames and are being flayed with whips. OTHERS are
tied to posts, apparently awaiting ordeal by fire.

There is a pile of DEAD BODIES at the end of the
courtyard. As LOKI is hustled across and into the Main
Hall, he just glimpses some STRANGE FIGURES who emerge
from the smoke of a pyre to fling some more dead
bodies on the pile. The FIGURES look almost surreal
... huge creatures with a man's body and a dog's head.
LOKI draws his breath in but has no time to look more
closely as he is pushed into the Main Hall.

18 **EXT.   HALFDAN'S HALL   DAY**

ANGLE ON HALFDAN THE BLACK, surrounded by two
ADVISORS.

He is a surprisingly amiable character. Before him a
WRETCHED FARMER, THORD ANDRESSON, is pinioned between
two GUARDS. His WIFE and CHILDREN are being held
behind him.

>   HALFDAN
>   Look, I'm not an unreasonable man,
>   (more)

(CONTINUED)

                         HALFDAN (CONT.)
               Thord Andresson, but this is the
               second chance I've given you ...

                         THORD ANDRESSON
               But I'm a poor man.

                         HALFDAN
               It's not just me - a lot of people
               depend on this money.

The advisors nod.

               I really *can't* give you a third
               chance ...

HALFDAN nods and the WRETCHED FARMER is hustled away.
His WIFE and CHILDREN scream.

                         THORD
                         (yelling)
               Take *all* my sheep!

                         HALFDAN
                         (with a charming
                         smile)
               I shall. Thank you ...

                         WIFE
               No! No! Thord!

                         CHILDREN
               Daddy!

They are all hustled past. HALFDAN shakes his head
sadly.

                         HALFDAN
               If only they'd think ahead. I *wish*
               they would.

The GUARD marches LOKI up to HALFDAN's throne.

HALFDAN smiles.

                         HALFDAN
               Ah! The blacksmith's assistant from
               Ravensfjord ...

As LOKI stands before HALFDAN, GUARDS keep presenting

(CONTINUED)

wretched PRISONERS to HALFDAN.

>   HALFDAN
>   (looking a prisoner
>   up and down)
>   Garrotting.

HALFDAN nods and PRISONER 1 is hustled off.

>   PRISONER 1
>   But, lord –

PRISONER 2 is brought forward by GUARD 2.

>   LOKI
>   My lord, Halfdan the Black.

>   HALFDAN
>   You've brought me more swords?
>   (to GUARD 2)
>   Beheading.

>   PRISONER 2
>   No! No! No!

>   LOKI
>   I bring more than swords. I bring a
>   warning from my master.

>   HALFDAN
>   A warning?
>   (to GUARD 3)
>   Flayed alive.

>   PRISONER 3
>   No! Listen! Please! It's all a
>   mistake! I can pay tomorrow! No!
>   Help!

He is dragged off.

>   LOKI
>   Erik and the men of Ravensfjord are
>   setting off to cross the Western
>   Ocean.

>   HALFDAN
>   Lucky things! *I* could do with a
>   holiday, I can tell you ... all this
>   (more)

(CONTINUED)

> HALFDAN (CONT.)
> financial work gives me a headache ...
>> (to GUARD 4)
> Flayed alive, garrotted, and *then*
> beheaded.

> PRISONER 4
> NO! NO! NO! I'm *not* Hildir
> Eysteinsson! I'm Hjalti Skeggjason!
> You've got the wrong man!

> LOKI
>> (ignoring the
>> PRISONER's screams)
> They seek to drive Fenrir the Wolf
> from the sky ... to wake the Gods and
> bring the Age of Ragnarok to an end.

HALFDAN'S ADVISORS suddenly show intense interest.

> GISLI ODDSSON
> *End* Ragnarok?

> EILIF THE RICH
> Who do they think they are?

> HALFDAN
>> (to GUARD 5)
> Just cut off his hand.

> PRISONER 5
> Thank you! Oh, thanks my merciful
> lord! Thank you a million thank-yous!
> Cut them *both* off if you want ...

PRISONER 5 is hustled off in a flurry of gratitude.

> HALFDAN
> And why should *you* tell me this?

> LOKI
> Because, my lord, my livelihood
> depends on it ... Like yours ...

The ADVISORS glance uneasily at HALFDAN, unsure how he
will react to this potential insult. LOKI himself
feels he may have gone too far. But HALFDAN smiles
condescendingly.

(CONTINUED)

> HALFDAN
> Besides ... were anything to happen
> to your master ... you would take
> over as blacksmith at Ravensfjord ...

LOKI smiles. HALFDAN and he understand each other
perfectly.

19 EXT.   GOLDEN DRAGON   DAY

ERIK and his MEN getting into the Golden Dragon.

ERIK notices THORFINN and SVEN quarreling over LEIF
THE LUCKY.

> ERIK
>
> Hey, you two! What's going on?

> SVEN
> I was sitting there.

> LEIF
> No, you weren't.

> THORFINN
> Leif's sitting here. I need a bit of
> luck.

> LEIF
> See.

> SVEN
> Look, I bagged it last week.

> ERIK
> It doesn't matter *where* you sit!

> SVEN
> Yes, it does! We could be at sea for
> months.

> ERIK
> Well, what difference does it make
> where you're *sitting*?

> SVEN
> I don't want to have to sit next to
> Snorri all that time.

(CONTINUED)

SVEN nods toward SNORRI THE MISERABLE - an Eeyore of a
Viking if ever there were one.

> SNORRI
> Thank you *very* much indeed.

> ERIK
> Now stop it!

> SNORRI
> It's *so* nice to feel wanted.

> ERIK
> Leif, you sit there. Sven, you sit
> there. Harald, you'd better sit over
> there ...

> SNORRI
> Trust me to get the missionary.

Suddenly ERIK notices SVEN'S FATHER climbing aboard.

> ERIK
> What are *you* doing here?

> SVEN'S DAD
> You may need a *real* Berserk.

> SVEN
> I *am* one, Dad!

> ERIK
> We haven't got a spare place.

> IVAR
> He can have my place. I don't want to
> go anyway.

> ERIK
> Well, you *are*!

> SVEN
> Bjorn's not. He could have Bjorn's
> place.

> ERIK
> What's the matter with Bjorn?

(CONTINUED)

> THORFINN
> Nothing ... Halfdan the Black chopped
> his hand off last night.

> ERIK
> *He* was lucky ...
> (to SVEN'S DAD)
> Sit there.

> THORFINN
> You can't have Sven's father sitting
> next to Sven. They'll argue the whole
> time.

> ERIK
> That's true.
> (to SVEN)
> *You'd* better sit there.
> (to SVEN'S DAD)
> You there, and Ornulf there.

> SNORRI
> Now you've got all the big ones on
> one side.

ERIK looks around. It is true that all the TALL BURLY
ONES are on one side.

> ERIK
> All right, you go there. You, here ...

SVEN'S DAD and ORNULF swap places.

> SVEN'S DAD
> Ohh! I wanted to sit next to Leif.

> ERIK
> Shut up. You there. You there and you
> there.

IVAR and ORNULF swap places.

ERIK surveys this re-arrangement.

> ERIK
> That's better.

> SNORRI
> Now you've got all the ones with
> (more)

(CONTINUED)

> SNORRI (CONT.)
> beards on one side and all the
> moustaches on the other.

This is true.

> ERIK
> It doesn't matter.

They start to haul the sail up. Ropes are released.
The boat rocks.

20 EXT.   QUAYSIDE AND SHIP   DAY

Suddenly a VOICE cuts through the CROWD. It is ERIK'S
MUM.

> ERIK'S MUM
> Wait! Wait! Wait!

> ERIK
> What is it?
> (he is clearly a
> little embarrassed)

> ERIK'S MUM
> Here, Son.

She tries to hand ERIK what looks unmistakably like a
pillow. ERIK is dumbfounded.

> ERIK'S MUM
> Your father always made sure he could
> rest his head at night.

ERIK is mortified. The OTHERS snigger, though not
without some sympathy for ERIK. They've *all* been
embarrassed by their mums at some time or other.

> ERIK
> I can't take *that* on a voyage!

> ERIK's MUM
> It was your father's!

ERIK will find it hard to refuse now. But he
hesitates.

(CONTINUED)

> ERIK'S MUM
> It was the pillow *he* took with him.
> He said it once saved his life.

ERIK reluctantly takes the precious object. His MOTHER kisses him. ERIK goes to his place, and tries to stuff the pillow into his sea chest. It won't fit.

EVERYONE has fallen silent now. The RELATIVES stand helpless on the shore as the Golden Dragon starts to drift away from them.

The VIKINGS sit in their places, hands on the oars, looking back at their LOVED ONES.

ERIK stands at the prow of the Golden Dragon. For a moment he thinks he sees the GIRL HE KILLED, standing white in death, the spear wound still fresh. ERIK raises his hand in a half-goodbye.

ANGLE ON the LOVED ONES, now the GIRL is no longer there. They, too, half-raise their hands.

CLOSE ON ERIK. He suddenly turns into CAMERA and gives a shout:

> ERIK
> Huuup!

A LONG SHOT of the Golden Dragon as all the oars go up vetically.

> ERIK
> Ahhhh!

The oars go down into the water, and the Golden Dragon commences her voyage.

IVAR THE BONELESS starts to drum out the rhythm.

21 EXT.   THE FJORD   DAY

A WIDE SHOT of Golden Dragon being rowed down the fjord.

                                              CUT TO:

The mouth of the fjord as the Golden Dragon emerges.

                                        (CONTINUED)

ANGLE ON ERIK at the prow - the breeze catches his hair.

ERIK raises his hand. They stop rowing and raise the mast and sail. The sail catches the offshore breeze and billows out.

22 EXT.   MOUTH OF FJORD/OPEN SEA   DAY

A LONG SHOT from behind a spit of land. Golden Dragon sailing off on the horizon.

23 EXT.   HALFDAN'S SHIP   DAY

Suddenly a SKULL slides silently across the screen, CLOSE-UP to CAMERA. It is one of HALFDAN's contorted skeletons. Then the back of a steel and leather helmet. The CAMERA stays with this helmet as it turns to reveal the visage of HALFDAN THE BLACK, or else a black sail blots out the scene. PAN DOWN onto CLOSE-UP of HALFDAN.

24 EXT.   GOLDEN DRAGON AT SEA   DAY

ANGLE ON ERIK feeling seasick. CAMERA TRACKS past him to pick up various members of the crew. IVAR is on a bucket having a quiet crap. SVEN'S DAD and LEIF are playing dice. KEITEL is watching. SVEN is feeling seasick. BJARNI and a NAMELESS HERO are cooking over a fire in a cauldron suspended from a contraption. ORNULF is fishing. The oars are stacked in high racks along the side of the ship.

SNORRI is feeling queasy and gazing gloomily at the receding coastline of Iceland. THANGBRAND is sitting near him and feeling extremely queasy.

> SNORRI
> Have a good look ... that's the last
> we'll see of old Norway.

SNORRI is desperately trying to control his insides.

> SNORRI
> Goodbye, home ... goodbye, family ...
> goodbye, loved ones ...
>   (more)

(CONTINUED)

                          SNORRI (CONT.)
                      (he starts to throw
                      up)
            Goodbye, lunch ...

                          THANGBRAND
            Oh! Shut up.

A wave of nausea sweeps over them. HARALD THE
MISSIONARY puts his arm around SNORRI.

                          HARALD
            You know, my son, our lord said ...

                          SNORRI
            Your lord.

                          HARALD
            Quite ... *my* lord ... said: "The
            Prayer of Faith shall save the sick."

                          SNORRI
            I hope the Dragon of the North Sea
            gets *you and* your lord.

HARALD THE MISSIONARY gives him a condescending smile
and a weary shake of the head. He knows the Dragon of
the North Sea does not exist.

                          HARALD
            Darkness and ignorance ...

ANGLE ON THORFINN SKULL-SPLITTER and SVEN, who is
feeling none too good.

                          SVEN
                      (keeping a wave of
                      nausea down)
            It's not so bad when you're rowing.

                          THORFINN SKULL-SPLITTER
            That's right.

                          SVEN THE BERSERK
            I want to die.

                          IVAR THE BONELESS
            Uh oh!

IVAR suddenly jumps up and pukes over the side. This

                                        (CONTINUED)

is too much for SNORRI and he follows suit. Mass puking
breaks out all over the boat.

ANGLE ON KEITEL BLACKSMITH. He looks around at his
preoccupied SHIPMATES, and it slowly dawns on him that
this might be the moment to try a little sabotage.

He goes to the ship's lodestone, which is hanging from
the mast.

KEITEL glances around. No one is looking, but this
sort of covert behavior goes against his normally
sunny and open disposition.

> KEITEL
> (to himself)
> The Blacksmith's Code ...

He steels himself, takes down the lodestone, and holds
it. It points "North."

He snaps out the piece of metal in the base and throws
it over the side.

KEITEL hangs it up again on the mast.

25 **EXT.   STERN   GOLDEN DRAGON AT SEA   DAY**

There is no wind. The sails flap idly.

IVAR is in the stern leaning over the side, looking
very green. THORFINN looms up behind him with a
malevolent grin.

> THORFINN
> You all right?

> IVAR
> No, I'm not.

> THORFINN
> You don't need to feel bad about
> being seasick, you know.

> IVAR
> How can you help feeling bad when
> you're seasick?

(CONTINUED)

                          THORFINN
          I mean, many of the greatest sailors
          were.

Pause.

                          IVAR
                     (he's heard this
                     before)
          I know. I know.

                          THORFINN
          Olaf Tryggvason used to throw up on
          every single voyage ... the whole
          time ... non-stop ... puke ... puke
          ... puke.

                          IVAR
          Look! I don't feel *bad* about it. I
          just feel *ill*.

Pause.

                          THORFINN
          He used to puke in his sleep.

                          IVAR
          Bastard.

He throws up.

Meanwhile ERIK has joined them. He is staring fixedly
at something on the horizon. ERIK nudges THORFINN.

                          ERIK
          Thorfinn ... look over there.

THORFINN looks up and sees what ERIK has seen on the
horizon. On the horizon a sinister black sail is
following them. There is a roll of distant thunder.
ERIK looks up at the sky. THORFINN grins with evil
pleasure. He smells a fight. IVAR takes one look and
throws up again.

ERIK turns to the crew.

                          ERIK
          Break out the oars!

THORFINN's smile disappears and he spins around to

                                        (CONTINUED)

confront ERIK.

> THORFINN
> What are you talking about?

> ERIK
> (to his reluctant
> crew)
> Come on, move it!

ANGLE ON CREW. Most are being seasick. They look up.

> MORD FIDDLE
> We've only just started cooking
> lunch.

The CREW glance at MORD FIDDLE and then turn and throw
up again.

> ERIK
> Move it!

Reluctantly the CREW take up their rowing positions.

THORFINN buttonholes ERIK (except of course he doesn't
have any buttonholes).

> THORFINN
> It's Halfdan the Black!

> ERIK
> I know. Snorri! Get your oar out!

SNORRI is sitting in position but without his oar.

KEITEL has meanwhile joined them. He, too, stares at
the horizon. He is a little puzzled by this turn of
events. LOKI has said nothing about HALFDAN coming
after them.

> KEITEL
> (uneasily)
> Do you suppose he wants to stop us
> waking the Gods?

ERIK looks at KEITEL with a certain amount of
contempt. KEITEL is not reknowned even amongst these
Vikings for his brain power.

(CONTINUED)

                              ERIK
                   What do you think?

                             KEITEL
                        (feigns innocence)
                   How could he know ... unless ...

KEITEL stops in mid-sentence as he realizes it must be
LOKI's doing. ERIK looks at him thinking "unless
what?"

                            THORFINN
                          (scornfully)
                   So, are you going to run away from
                   him, Erik?

ERIK turns on THORFINN.

                              ERIK
                   Row, Thorfinn Skull-Splitter.

THORFINN hesitates.

                              ERIK
                   And you, Keitel Blacksmith.

                             KEITEL
                   But ...

KEITEL shrugs and turns to take up his rowing
position. He is still a little confused by this turn
of events. Maybe the first doubts about LOKI have been
sown.

ERIK confronts THORFINN.

                              ERIK
                   I gave an order. Or didn't you hear?

There is something about ERIK's manner that carries an
authority that THORFINN cannot argue with. He is
overcome by the strength of ERIK's will, and suddenly
turns and takes up his oar.

                              ERIK
                   Come on, Ivar.

ERIK manhandles IVAR over to his drum and thrusts his
drumsticks into his hands.

26 EXT.   THE OPEN SEA   DAY

   MONTAGE of shots of the two ships. HALFDAN THE BLACK's
   ship seems to be catching up with ERIK's.

   There is another roll of thunder. The sky begins to
   boil.

27 EXT.   GALLEY OF HALFDAN'S SHIP   DAY

   HALFDAN's ship. In contrast to ERIK's boat, HALFDAN's
   is a long mean-looking warship and it is painted all
   black. With a black sail. It looks very ominous, and
   it is certainly going *very* fast.

28 EXT.   GOLDEN DRAGON AT SEA   DAY

                    IVAR
               (still feeling ill)
          I want to die ...
               (then suddenly
               remembering they are
               being chased)
          No, I don't!

                    ERIK
          Row! Row! Row!

   IVAR tries to get into the new rhythm, but has a bit
   of difficulty. ERIK peers back at HALFDAN's ship.

                    ERIK
               (to himself)
          It's impossible ... no one can row at
          that speed ...

   ERIK turns and sees mist ahead. He leans on the
   steering oar.

29 EXT.   GOLDEN DRAGON IN MIST   DAY

   Suddenly Golden Dragon glides into a thick sea mist.
   There is a tremendous roll of thunder very close. All
   the VIKINGS look scared. ERIK, however, grins.

                    ERIK
          Row! Row! Row!

                                        (CONTINUED)

29 CONTINUED:

He doubles the speed. The drum beats faster.

> SVEN's DAD
> (shouts out angrily)
> We can't keep this up.

Suddenly ERIK lays his hand on the drum and silences it.

> ERIK
> Oars up!

The VIKINGS all lift up their oars in unison. Then ERIK leans on the steering oar and Golden Dragon curves around in a great arc through the mist. ERIK beckons everyone to keep quiet.

30 EXT.   ANOTHER PART OF THE MIST   DAY

Another shot of Golden Dragon appearing and disappearing in the mist.

31 EXT.   HALFDAN'S SHIP IN MIST   DAY

Then a shot of HALFDAN THE BLACK's ship entering the mist.

HALFDAN's boat curves around in the opposite direction from ERIK's.

32 EXT.   GOLDEN DRAGON IN MIST   DAY

ERIK has stopped the MEN rowing, they are all holding their breaths, and listening to the splashing of the Black Ship's oars and the beat of HALFDAN's drum getting more distant.

The MEN look at each other and smile. Only KEITEL seems less than pleased ... but as he catches someone's eye even he forces a smile.

FADE.

33 EXT.   GOLDEN DRAGON AMONGST THE MIST ISLANDS   DAY

                                                  FADE UP.

They are still drifting in the mist, when they pass
between two strange islands. SPOOKY MUSIC.

                        ERIK
              The Gates of the World ...

                        KEITEL
              What?

                        ERIK
              We have passed through the Gates of
              the World.
                        (he looks around at
                        the others)
              Now we are in the Unknown ...

                                                  FADE.

34 EXT.   GOLDEN DRAGON IN MIST   DAY

                                                  FADE UP.

Sometime later. ERIK has his fish-lodestone and is
trying the direction, but the lodestone is just
swinging around uselessly. After trying a few times,
ERIK gives up and throws the lodestone away into the
boat.

The MEN peer into the mist. They are lost.

Suddenly IVAR nudges SNORRI. They gape as the ship
drifts by a strange SHAPE in the mist. Nobody knows
what it could be but it looks like the leg of a huge
bird that just sticks out of the water and disappears
up in the mist. Nobody says anything.

On the other side a grotesque silhouette that could be
a narwhal swims past. The MUSIC underlines the magic
feeling of being in the unknown.

35 EXT.   GOLDEN DRAGON AND THE DRAGON   DAY

Golden Dragon drifts on and the mist gets thicker.
There is a crash of thunder. Then a series of flashes

                                              (CONTINUED)

51

lights up the mist around them. The VIKINGS are
uneasy.

Suddenly ERIK points above them. The OTHERS look up,
too. They *all* gasp.

>   ERIK
>   (hardly daring to
>   breathe)
> So *that* is what the sun looks like.

Above them hangs a luminous yellow globe, its light
just breaking through the mist.

>   VIKINGS
>   (to each other)
> The Sun! It's the Sun! Look!

>   SVEN's DAD
>   (in wonderment)
> I never thought I should live to see
> the Sun again.

>   HARALD
> Where?

The VIKINGS all gaze up above them in awe. HARALD
looks from one to the other and then tries to follow
their eyelines. He clearly can't see it. MAGIC MUSIC
fills the air.

Suddenly the "Sun" swoops off to one side and starts
swaying from one side to the other.

ERIK frowns.

>   ERIK
> Should the Sun do that?

KEITEL shrugs.

>   HARALD
> What are you looking at?

>   ERIK
> Look out!

>   VIKINGS
> Ah!

(CONTINUED)

The VIKINGS scream and flatten themselves against the
sides of the boat as the "Sun" suddenly lurches down
on them out of the sky revealing for the first time
that it is *not* the sun at all, but a huge MONSTER with
a long neck that disappears off into the mist, and a
glowing globe for a head, and huge chomping jaws.

The VIKINGS are, understandably, terrified.

>   VIKINGS
>   It's not the Sun! It's not the Sun!

>   HARALD THE MISSIONARY
>   What is it?

>   SNORRI
>   It's the Dragon of the North Sea!

>   HARALD THE MISSIONARY
>   (knowingly)
>   Ah! *That's* why I can't see it.

As the Dragon of the North Sea rises up again,
however, its jaw apparently drops off and falls to the
deck, and lands on SNORRI.

>   SNORRI
>   Aaah!

KEITEL nervously picks it up and holds it up for
everyone to see. It is a strand of sea-weed. The
VIKINGS are nonplussed. They look back at their now
jawless MONSTER.

>   THORFINN
>   Some dragon!

Suddenly there is an incredibly loud clap of thunder
and flames shoot out of the mist.

>   SVEN
>   Look out!

As ... unbelievably ... a huge monstrous visage looms
out of the mist ... it is a CREATURE FROM THE
NETHERMOST DEPTHS OF THE OCEAN ... it is white and
gelatinous and ugly beyond description - and the
incandescent globe is no more than a sprouting on the
end of its nose! The fire lights up the mist all
around and sends all the VIKINGS (and even HARALD THE

                                        (CONTINUED)

MISSIONARY) diving for the deck. Then the monstrous
head disappears back into the mist as quickly as it
came, taking its light with it ...

The VIKINGS are paralyzed with fear for one brief
moment.

> ERIK
> Row! ROW!

They all scramble and leap for the oars in a
determined hysteria.

IVAR the drummer, in his panic, has set a ridiculously
fast rate and nobody can keep up with it.

> ERIK
> Slower! Nobody can row at that speed!

> IVAR
> (hoarsely)
> Sorry!

> HARALD
> (shouts across to
> SVEN)
> What's all the panic about?

> SVEN
> (in panic, shouting
> back over his
> shoulder)
> The Dragon ...

HARALD gives a patronizing smile, and looks around at
the OTHERS shaking his head knowingly.

> HARALD
> Children afraid of the dark ...

They get themselves together and manage to row in
spite of their panic. But suddenly there is another
roar and flames shoot out of the mist and across the
deck of the Golden Dragon.

One man, ORNOLF FISHDRIVER, who hasn't had much to say
so far, is set on fire. Two OTHERS try to put him out.
Another, BJARNI JERUSALEM-FARER, who has had and will
have even less to say than ORNOLF FISHDRIVER, leaps
out of the way of the flames and falls over the side.

(CONTINUED)

ORNOLF dies.

> THORFINN
>> Man overboard!

THORFINN starts trying to fish him out.

IVAR has started to panic and is beating the drum too fast.

> ERIK
>> Slower! In ... Out ...

> IVAR
>> Sorry!

> SVEN
>> (his eyes showing
>> their whites)
> We're being attacked! KILL! KILL! KILL!

SVEN'S DAD rushes over to him, as low-key as ever.

> SVEN'S DAD
>> Not now, Sven ...

> SVEN
>> I must KILL! Kill!

> SVEN's DAD
>> It's no good going berserk against a dragon!

SVEN'S DAD slaps him about the face and eventually SVEN comes out of it.

There is another roar from the MONSTER now hidden in the mists once again—only the light glowing.

> ERIK
>> (to IVAR)
>> Faster!

> IVAR
>> (to himself)
>> Make your mind up.

ANGLE ON HARALD THE MISSIONARY praying earnestly.

                                        (CONTINUED)

> HARALD
> Oh Merciful Father, let these good
> men survive this fearful storm ...

> SNORRI
> It's not a storm! It's a dragon!

Suddenly the DRAGON's head appears out of the mists
above them once again.

Panic amongst the VIKINGS as some start to row faster
than others. Screams.

> ERIK
> Keep up the strike!

CLOSE-UP the DRAGON's jaws opening. Flames lick out,
and down the center of the vessel. Screams as the
VIKINGS leap out of the way. Three nameless HEROES
fall overboard. Various bits of the boat catch fire.

SVEN goes berserk again.

> SVEN
> KILL! KILL!

> SVEN'S DAD
> Stop it!

The DRAGON's eyes dilate and its jaws open.

The MEN throw themselves to the deck as if expecting
more fire.

But instead the CREATURE's fangs crash into the wood
of the stern of Golden Dragon.

> ERIK
> (who has grabbed a
> spare oar)
> ROW!

> SVEN
> DEATH!

> SVEN'S DAD
> Shut UP!

> ERIK
> Row!

(CONTINUED)

ERIK looks around at his terror-stricken crew. He
realizes this is an important moment. It is up to him
to save the situation. Suddenly an idea occurs to him,
as he catches sight of the pillow that his Mother gave
him.

> ERIK
>> Keep rowing!

ERIK dashes to his sea chest under the mast and pulls
out the pillow.

> THORFINN
> Erik! Row! What are you doing?

> ERIK
>> (holding up the
>> pillow)
> It saved my father!

ERIK starts to shin up the mast.

> SNORRI
>> Barmy.

SVEN'S DAD is desperately holding SVEN back.

> SVEN'S DAD
> *Hold* it! *Hold* it in!

> SVEN
> DEATH TO DRAGONS!

> ERIK
>> Row!

> SNORRI
> Has anyone told him we've got a
> dragon eating our boat?

Despite all their efforts at rowing they cannot break
free of the MONSTER's jaws. The light sways above
them.

> HARALD
> Oh Lord, abate this terrible storm!
> *Please*!

SVEN'S DAD lets go of SVEN and takes up his oar. SVEN
charges recklessly at the DRAGON's jaws. But a bolt of

(CONTINUED)

fire suddenly sends him reeling back, and his jerkin
in flames. At the same time, the fourth (and last)
NAMELESS HERO falls overboard.

HARALD throws his cassock over SVEN and puts the fire
out.

The DRAGON gives another roar and scrunches its jaws
further up the deck of the Golden Dragon. Its snout is
buried in the sails.

ERIK has reached the top of the mast and is now right
up with the incandescent globe on the end of the long
stalk that grows from the CREATURE's nose.

> ERIK
>
> All right, Wart-Nose!

With this cry, ERIK grabs the stalk where it joins the
globe, and swings up onto the CREATURE's nose.

SVEN, who is extremely singed, breaks free of the sack
and recommences his attack on the MONSTER. He starts
belaboring one of its teeth with his sword. The tooth
rings out hollowly, and sparks fly.

> SVEN
> Red mist!

ERIK looks down at SVEN in despair. SVEN'S DAD shuts
his eyes.

ANGLE ON HARALD THE MISSIONARY who is going around to
the MEN offering his Bible.

> HARALD
> It's at times like this that you'll
> find this book *most* useful, you
> know ...

KEITEL takes the Bible from him and hits him over the
head with it.

> KEITEL
> Row! You idiot!

> CUT TO:

The MONSTER's eyes are dilating wildly as they try to

> (CONTINUED)

focus on the tiny figure of ERIK on its snout.

>   ERIK
>   Try this for size!

ERIK shoves the pillow up one of the DRAGON's
nostrils.

>   ERIK
>   (almost hysterical)
>   How d'you like that?

>   CUT TO:

SNORRI watching ERIK incredulously. He shakes his
head.

>   SNORRI
>   His father went crazy, too ... used
>   to take 40 winks in the middle of a
>   battle ...

THORFINN frowns - he has a glimmering of an idea of
what ERIK is doing.

ANGLE ON ERIK who has now plunged his sword right
through the pillow in the DRAGON's nostril. The DRAGON
goes cross-eyed trying to see what's going on on its
snout.

>   ERIK
>   Now ... a deep breath.

The DRAGON seems to be deliberately holding its
breath. But its snout wrinkles as if it is starting
to tickle.

>   ERIK
>   Go on! Breathe in, you Cod-Brain!

Meanwhile the DRAGON's tongue suddenly licks out
around its tooth. SVEN instantly slices through it
with his sword. The bright blood spurts, like bursting
a sausage. The DRAGON gives an agonized roar and a
sharp intake of breath. The few feathers that have now
leaked out from the pillow are instantly sucked inside
and the whole pillow disappears right up the DRAGON's
nose.

For a moment EVERYONE holds their breath.

>   (CONTINUED)

35 CONTINUED:

The DRAGON's eyes dilate wildly.

Then it wrinkles its snout again.

Then it starts what is unmistakeably a sneeze.

                         DRAGON
         Ah ... ah ... ah ...

                         ERIK
         Hold TIGHT!

                         DRAGON
         Ah ... ah ... ah ...

ERIK leaps back across the mast.

                         DRAGON
         CHOO!

CLOSE-UP of the wind and feathers coming out of the
DRAGON's nostrils.

CLOSE-UP of the blast of air hitting all the VIKINGS
at once and blowing their hair straight out behind
them, and covering them in feathers.

EVERYONE is disgusted by the DRAGON's breath.

                         SNORRI
         Urgh! What's it been eating?

ANGLE ON the sail of the Golden Dragon filling.

SHOT from Golden Dragon of the DRAGON disappearing
rapidly back into the mist as the boat is blown into
the air.

36 EXT.   GOLDEN DRAGON   FLYING   DAY

Suddenly the mist clears from them. They all look up
at ERIK and cheer.

ANGLE ON ERIK. He doesn't look too happy.

KEITEL looks down and frowns. So does IVAR. He
boggles.

                                        (CONTINUED)

                                        CUT TO:

A SHOT over their shoulders and see that the sea is
far below them.

They are flying.

                                        CUT TO:

A WIDE SHOT of Golden Dragon flying through the air.

                                        CUT TO:

The ship's deck. IVAR screams and leaps to his feet.
The OTHERS all rush to the side to look, too.

                    ERIK
          No! No! Get back!

Unfortunately they all rush to the *same* side and the
boat tips over with far more instability than when it
is in the water.

LEIF and THANGBRAND are catapulted down into the sea.
We watch them descend into tiny dots and tiny unheard
splashes below.

                    THORFINN
          Who was that?

                    SNORRI
          Leif the Lucky.

OTHERS are almost falling out. They scramble and are
pulled back in. There is renewed panic.

                    ERIK
          Get back!

Poor ERIK is still up the mast but has been dislodged
and is now hanging on by his hands, dangling over the
open sea.

Some of the MEN - THORFINN and SVEN THE BERSERK
amongst them — are hauling themselves up the almost
vertical slope of the deck, trying to redress the
balance.

                    KEITEL
          I can't hold on! I can't hold on!

                                        (CONTINUED)

KEITEL BLACKSMITH is hanging by one hand from the side of Golden Dragon.

SVEN worms his way along the edge – at great peril to himself — and grabs KEITEL's wrist just as his fingers slip.

> KEITEL
>
> Aaagh!

> SVEN
>
> Got you!

KEITEL looks up into SVEN's eyes. He is totally at SVEN's mercy. What thoughts are going through his mind? How is he going to betray SVEN in the future if he is rescued? Guilt suddenly overwhelms him.

> KEITEL
>
> Let me go, Sven.

> SVEN
>
> What are you talking about?

> KEITEL
>
> I'm not worth risking your life for.

> SVEN
>
> I've got you, Keitel Blacksmith. If you go ... I go too ...

> KEITEL
>
> For your own sake ... for the others ... I ...

> SVEN
>
> Hang on ...

The boat begins to right itself just as ERIK finally can't hold on any more, and he plummets, straight into the ship and through the bottom up to his waist. His legs dangle.

At the same moment the prow of the boat tips and suddenly they are plummeting down toward the ocean.

> SNORRI
>
> Here we go!

37 **EXT.** **GOLDEN DRAGON** **SINKING** **DAY**

They hit the water with an almighty splash and spray,
and all the COMRADES are thrown into a heap. ERIK is
pushed free and water gushes up through the hole he
has made.

The REST OF THE CREW look on as if numbed by this
fresh disaster.

>   SNORRI
>   First we're flying — now we're
>   sinking!

>   ERIK
>   Well, come on!

He whisks off his helmet and starts bailing. All
follow suit.

NIGHT FALLS.

38 **EXT.** **GOLDEN DRAGON** **SINKING** **NIGHT**

The VIKINGS are still bailing out but the water is up
to their thighs.

>   IVAR THE BONELESS
>   Who are we fooling? It's hopeless!

IVAR flings down the helmet with which he's been
bailing. The OTHERS look at each other and pause.
CAMERA PANS amongst the somber faces of the MEN. They
are reconciled to the fact that they are going to
drown.

>   HARALD THE MISSIONARY
>   (hopelessly)
>   Let's sing something!

>   SNORRI
>   Anyone know any good drowning songs?

The suggestion falls flat.

>   ERIK
>   Listen! Maybe we won't get to
>   (more)

                                        (CONTINUED)

                          ERIK (CONT.)
          Hy-Brasil! Maybe we won't find the
          Horn Resounding ... but at least
          we've tried ... and at least we shall
          have died like men.

                          SNORRI
          Like fish.

                          SVEN
          Shut up.

                          THORFINN
                (raising his sword)
          Erik's right! We'll all meet in
          Valhalla.

                          IVAR
          I don't want to die!

                          HARALD THE MISSIONARY
          Isn't there *anybody* who'd like to be
          christened before we go down?

Silence. A distinct lack of enthusiasm.

                          HARALD
          It can't do you any *harm* ...

                          SVEN'S DAD
          What do we have to do?

                          HARALD
          Nothing ... I just immerse you in
          water ...

                          THORFINN & OTHERS
          Get lost ...

The ship creaks and starts to go under. ERIK looks at
his MEN. Tears in his eyes. Then he picks up his
sword. The OTHERS follow suit.

                          ERIK
          Don't let me drown, Thorfinn!

Water begins pouring over the low sides of the boat.

                          THORFINN
          Till we meet in Valhalla.

                                        (CONTINUED)

They all prepare to run each other through. The boat
sinks rapidly beneath the waves.

> IVAR THE BONELESS
> I'm too young! Oh, Odin! Not me!
> Please not me! Perhaps I'd rather
> drown ...

> HARALD THE MISSIONARY
> I do *wish* you'd let me convert you.

Then ERIK pauses in his attempt to kill THORFINN and
looks around. The ship has sunk, but the prow and the
stern posts are still sticking up out of the water,
and the VIKINGS themselves are only up to their
chests.

> ERIK
> How deep *is* the ocean?

> THORFINN
> Very deep ... usually ...

The realization gradually dawns on the VIKINGS that
they're not going to sink any more.

> ERIK
> Wait! Nobody kill anybody!

39 **EXT.   OPEN SEA   DAY**

The sun rising above the horizon of the sea.

The VIKINGS waking up are standing with just their
heads and shoulders sticking up above the water. All
they can see is an endless expanse of sea ... but on
the horizon, inching its way above it ... the Sun!

> THORFINN
> What is it?

> IVAR THE BONELESS
> (he panics and
> turns)
> It's the Dragon again.

> ERIK
> No ... no it isn't ...

(CONTINUED)

65

More MAGICAL SHOTS of the sunrise. IVAR has turned and is gasping and speechless.

> ERIK
> Look, the sky is blue ...

They all stand gazing in awe.

> SVEN'S DAD
> The Sun! That's it!

IVAR, meanwhile, is recovering from the amazement that has immobilized him. He taps ERIK on the shoulder. ERIK turns and gasps.

> ERIK
> Look!

40 EXT.   THE SHORE OF HY-BRASIL   DAY

They all turn to see that they are standing in the sea by the shore of a green and pleasant land. The boat has sunk in the shallow waters of a natural harbor. There is a slight pause, then they all look at each other and let out a whoop of triumph.

> VIKINGS
> Yeaaaah!

And they all promptly disappear under the waves! There is a pause, during which a great deal of underwater scrabbling about makes us wonder what is going on. Then the VIKINGS all suddenly reappear wearing their helmets and brandishing their swords, axes and so on. They are armed to the teeth and ready to go. They wade ashore, and find themselves in a beautiful country with Greek temples standing on hills ... Paradise! A city of white is set in the distance.

41 EXT.   OUTSIDE THE CITY OF HY-BRASIL   DAY

The VIKINGS are climbing up a beautiful hill beside the sea.

Sheep are grazing peacefully, and there under a weeping willow, lies the most beautiful GIRL. She is raven-haired, scantily dressed and fast asleep.

(CONTINUED)

The VIKINGS approach her with trepidation, their
swords and axes drawn. They glance around uneasily.

> SNORRI
> (whispers)
> She's got no clothes on!

> THORFINN
> It's disgusting.

> ERIK
> Get her weapons.

SVEN kneels quietly beside the GIRL. She stirs. SVEN
freezes. The OTHERS look round fearfully.

> SVEN
> (whispers)
> She hasn't got any!

> ERIK
> (incredulous)
> She *must* have a knife or something ...

But they look. She hasn't.

> THORFINN
> What kind of a place *is* this?

> IVAR THE BONELESS
> P...p... perhaps they've got weapons
> we haven't even dreamed of ...

Suddenly the GIRL stirs again in her sleep.

The VIKINGS retreat several paces and grip their
weapons, and glance around as if expecting an ambush.

> THORFINN
> Let's hack her to pieces.

> ERIK
> No.

> KEITEL
> Well, what else do we do?

> ERIK
> How about making friends?

(CONTINUED)

                        SVEN
                 (with disgust)
      "Friends"?

                     VIKINGS
      Eurrgh!

                     ERIK
     What's wrong with making friends?

                   THORFINN
     You don't go through all the
     hardships of an ocean voyage to make
     "friends."

                     SVEN
     We can make "friends" at home ...

This conversation has awakened the GIRL.

                     AUD
     Welcome!

The VIKINGS react with terror, take a step back and
raise their swords and axes.

                     ERIK
     What did you say?

                     AUD
     I said you are welcome.

                     ERIK
               (suspiciously)
     Welcome?

                     AUD
     Well, of course. We always welcome
     friends.

The VIKINGS look at each other and at their swords.
They don't think they look that much like friends
themselves.

                     ERIK
     How d'you *know* we're "friends"?

                     AUD
     Well, *everyone* is friends here on
     Hy-Brasil.

                              (CONTINUED)

> SVEN
> Hy-Brasil?

> ERIK
> Is *this* Hy-Brasil?

> AUD
> Well, of course.

> ERIK
> We've arrived on the Dragon's Breath!

Much jubilation and hugging and waving their swords in
the air and mock fighting.

AUD, however, reacts to all this with horror.

> AUD
> Please! Please! What are those?

> ERIK
> What are what?

> AUD
> Those things in your hands.

> ERIK
> These? What are *these*? They're
> swords.

AUD instantly recoils in horror.

> AUD
> Oh no! NO! Put them down! PUT THEM
> DOWN!

The VIKINGS gradually cease their mock battles and
turn to look at AUD with incredulity.

> ERIK
> What's the matter?

> AUD
> PLEASE! You don't know what you're
> doing!

> ERIK
> What?

                              AUD
              Put them down!
                        (to ERIK)
              PLEASE make them put them down.

                              THORFINN
              Why?

                              OTHERS
              Yes, why?

                              AUD
              Why?

                              ERIK
              Yes.

                              AUD
              But surely you know ... ?

                              VIKINGS
              Er ... n ... no ...

                              ERIK
              Know what?

42 INT.   **THE KING'S HALL   HY-BRASIL   DAY**

A Big CLOSE-UP of KING ARNULF.

                         KING ARNULF
              The wonderful blessing under which we
              live here on Hy-Brasil?

The KING beams. The VIKINGS shift uneasily. They look
out of place and extremely scruffy in the midst of the
scantily dressed COURTIERS of Hy-Brasil. AUD sits
beside her FATHER the KING.

                         ERIK
              No ... we don't ...

                         KING ARNULF
              The Gods decreed that if ever sword
              spills human blood upon these shores,
              the whole of Hy-Brasil will sink
              beneath the waves.

KING ARNULF beams rapturously at the VIKINGS,

                                          (CONTINUED)

expecting them to be overjoyed. Instead they are
horrified. AUD catches ERIK's eye and gives him a
dangerously slow wink.

> THORFINN
> That's terrible!

> ERIK
> You mean if just *one person* gets
> killed?

> KING ARNULF
> Yes!

>> (he thinks: "Isn't
>> it wonderful?")

The VIKINGS look at each other, feeling they haven't
quite understood.

> THORFINN
> You mean ... you can't kill *anybody*?

> KING ARNULF
> Right! Isn't it wonderful?

The VIKINGS are nonplussed.

> THORFINN
> What? Not being able to kill anybody?

> KING ARNULF
> (bemused)
> Well, of course.

> ERIK
> (interested)
> How?

> KING ARNULF
> (explaining the
> obvious)
> Well ... for a start ... er ...
> there's no killing ...

> ERIK
> Well, *obviously* there's no killing.

> KING ARNULF
> Well ... ["Isn't it great?"]

(CONTINUED)

71

                         THORFINN
          But how d'you take revenge?

                          KEITEL
                        (guiltily)
          How do you punish people?

                          ERIK
                       (even more
                       interested)
          How do you *defend* yourselves?

                       KING ARNULF
                    (getting a little
                     irritated)
          We don't have to! We're all terribly
          nice to each other. Aren't we?

                          COURT
          Yes!

A pause of disbelief from the VIKINGS.

                          ERIK
          All the time?

                       KING ARNULF
          Well, of course! We *have* to be.

He turns and conducts the COURTIERS who chant in
unison:

                          COURT
          "Being nice to each other is what
          it's all about."

                       KING ARNULF
                    (rising as if to
                     sing)
          You see?
          We're terribly nice to each other
          We're friendly, bold and free.
          We never say anything nasty
          'Cause we dare not ...

                          COURT
                      (*almost* singing)
          No sirreeeee!

They hold the note while KING ARNULF looks at the
VIKINGS.

                                        (CONTINUED)

> KING ARNULF
> Would you like us to sing to you?

> ERIK
> That's very kind of you, but we're in
> rather a hurry ... We're ...

KING ARNULF stops the COURT holding the note.

> KING ARNULF
> What's the matter, don't you *want* to
> hear our singing?

> ERIK
> Oh ... well, yes, of course, it's
> just we're looking for the Horn
> Resounding and —

> KING ARNULF
> You don't think our singing's going
> to be good enough for you?

> ERIK
> Oh no no no! It's just the Horn
> Resounding is ...

> KING ARNULF
> A lot of people like our singing.

> ERIK
> I'm sure it's lovely.

> KING ARNULF
> But you don't want to hear it.

> ERIK
> (changing tack)
> No ... no ...
> (he looks at the
> others)
> We'd love to hear it. Wouldn't we?

> VIKINGS
> Oh ... yes.

> KING ARNULF
> Well, you'll have to ask us *really*
> nicely.

(CONTINUED)

> ERIK
> (realizes he has to
> be diplomatic)
> Er ... well ... we ... we ... would
> be *terribly* grateful if you ... all
> ... would sing for us.

> KING ARNULF
> You're just saying that.

> SVEN
> Well, of course he is!

> SVEN'S DAD
> Sh!

They restrain SVEN.

> ERIK
> Of course we're not; we'd genuinely
> like to hear you sing.

> KING ARNULF
> *Really*?

> ERIK
> Really.

> KING ARNULF
> And you're not just saying it because
> you think we want you to?

ERIK swallows hard. HARALD THE MISSIONARY shakes his
head.

> ERIK
> No.
> (he bites the lie)

> KING ARNULF
> Right! Summon the musicians! We'll do
> the one that goes "TUM-TUM-TUM-TUM-
> TI-TUM-TUM."

> COURT
> (disappointed)
> Oh ...

> CHAMBERLAIN
> *Really*?

(CONTINUED)

                         KING ARNULF
                    (apologetically to
                         VIKINGS)
          It isn't the one we're *best* at.

                         CHAMBERLAIN
          Couldn't we do the one that goes
          "TUM-TI-TUM-TI-TUM-TI-TUM"?

The REST OF THE COURT look hopeful.

                         KING ARNULF
                      (whispering)
          Not when we've got guests.

                    VOICE FROM THE COURT
          How about the one that goes:
          "TI-TUM-TI-TUM-TI-TUM-TI-TI-TUM"?

                         KING ARNULF
          Don't be silly.

                         CHAMBERLAIN
          That was a stupid suggestion.

                           VOICE
          Sorry! I just thought they might like
          to hear something that we can do.

                          ANOTHER
          Yes! At least we know that one.

                      YET ANOTHER VOICE
          Nobody knows the "TUM-TUM-TUM-TUM
          -TI-TUM-TUM" one.

                      REST OF COURT
          No! Right! I agree!

                         ODD MAN OUT
          I do!

                      REST OF COURT
          Sh!

                      ANOTHER VOICE
          It's too difficult!

                         CHAMBERLAIN
          Sh!

                                        (CONTINUED)
                         75

> KING ARNULF
> All right. We'll do the one that goes
> "TI-TUM-TI-TUM-TI-TUM-TI-TI-TUM."
> Ah! The Musicians!

THE MUSICIANS are huge, unshaven, have broken noses,
tattoos, and are covered in black oil — like
mechanics. Their instruments are like heavy industrial
machinery, pushed in large vats of black oil that drip
all over the show.

> KING ARNULF
> Right ... Oh, dear ...
>> (he glances across
>> at the VIKINGS)
> I'm sure you're not going to like
> this ...

ERIK and the OTHERS smile reassuringly.

There is a lot of coughing. The KING raises his baton
and then brings it down, humming to himself as he does
so! There is a most awful din: caterwauling, crashing
and banging, whining, screaming ...

The VIKINGS look at each other, trying to pick out
some tune, but it's impossible.

IVAR THE BONELESS can't stop himself bursting out
laughing but ERIK glares at him. SVEN also gets the
giggles. KING ARNULF notices and bangs the throne for
silence.

Gradually the din stops.

> KING ARNULF
>> (tragically)
> We're just not a very musical
> nation ...

> ERIK
> No no ... It was very ... er ...
> nice.

> KING ARNULF
> Now I want you to be *absolutely*,
> totally, genuinely honest with me.
> Did you really, truly, honestly like
> it?

(CONTINUED)

ERIK thinks for some moments and then decides to make
a clean breast of it.

>   ERIK
>   No.

>   KING ARNULF
>   (becomes hysterical)
>   They didn't like it! Oh God! I want
>   to die!

The WHOLE COURT looks as if it's about to commit mass
hara-kiri, while the MUSICIANS look rather dangerous.

ERIK takes the moment to get down to business.

>   ERIK
>   Your majesty! We come from a world of
>   darkness, where Fenrir the Wolf
>   covers the sun, a world where men
>   live and die by the axe and by the
>   sword ...

>   KING ARNULF
>   Well, how d'you think *I* feel?

>   ERIK
>   The Gods are asleep, King Arnulf.

>   KING ARNULF
>   *You* try to be nice to people, when
>   they're rude about your singing ...

ERIK feels he is making a mess of all this diplomacy.

>   ERIK
>   We must find the Horn Resounding!

The KING glares at ERIK.

>   ERIK
>   Is it *here* in Hy-Brasil?

KING ARNULF thinks for a moment and then speaks.

>   KING ARNULF
>   I'll tell you what ...

>   ERIK
>   Yes?

>   (CONTINUED)

KING ARNULF hesitates — he bites his lip and then takes the plunge.

> KING ARNULF
> We'll do the one that goes
> "TUM-TUM-TUM-TUM-TI-TUM-TUM."
> Perhaps you'll like that better.

ERIK gives up.

A lot of throat clearing.

AUD, the KING'S DAUGHTER, gives ERIK another dangerously slow wink.

43 EXT.   OUTSIDE THE PALACE   HY-BRASIL   DAY

The terrible "music" starts up.

> FADE.

44 EXT.   THE SHORE   HY-BRASIL   DAY

> FADE UP

ANGLE ON Golden Dragon, now afloat once more, riding at anchor in the bay. IVAR is standing on guard in it.

45 EXT.   THE OPEN SEA   DAY

ANGLE ON the HORIZON. From around a spit of land comes HALFDAN THE BLACK'S ship. THREATENING MUSIC.

46 INT.   PRINCESS AUD'S BEDCHAMBER   DAY

ANGLE ON ERIK. He is deeply in love. He is also in bed with the KING's nubile daughter, AUD.

> UAD
> Have you ever felt like this about
> anyone else?

> ERIK
> What ... you mean "got into bed with"
> them?

(CONTINUED)

> AUD
> No, of course not, silly — I mean
> *felt* like this about them?

> ERIK
> You mean ... you *have* got into bed
> with somebody else?

> AUD
> No, I mean have you ever felt that
> for the first time in your life you'd
> met someone you could believe in with
> your whole heart ... someone whose
> goals suddenly seem to be *your* goals
> ... whose dreams seem to be *your*
> dreams?

> ERIK
> *Have* you ever been to bed with anyone
> else?

> AUD
> What does that matter? But you've ...
> you've ... *felt* like this before ...

> ERIK
> It was different ...

> AUD
> (could be HELGA just
> for this and her
> next speech)
> What was she like?

> ERIK
> Oh ... oh, I didn't know her very
> well ...

> AUD
> (or HELGA)
> But you *loved* her all the same ...

> ERIK
> We never went to bed together.

> AUD
> Why do you go on about that? What
> does it matter?

(CONTINUED)

>   ERIK
>   You've been to bed with somebody
>   else, haven't you?

>   AUD
>   I've never *loved* anybody!

>   ERIK
>   *I've* never been to bed with anybody!

Suddenly there is a banging on the door.

>   KING ARNULF (V.O.)
>   Aud!

>   AUD
>   Ah! It's my father!

>   KING ARNULF (V.O.)
>   Open up! I know you're in there!

Suddenly the note from IVAR's horn rings out across
the bay. ERIK rushes to the window and looks out.

>   ERIK
>   Oh, no! Halfdan!

47 **EXT.   VIEW FROM PRINCESS AUD'S BEDCHAMBER   DAY**

We see the Black Ship approaching.

Banging on door.

48 **INT.   PRINCESS AUD'S BEDCHAMBER   DAY**

>   KING ARNULF (V.O.)
>   Aud! You've got someone in there
>   again, haven't you?

ERIK gives her a sharp look.

>   AUD
>   Quick! Throw this over you!

She throws a shabby bit of cloth over ERIK and at that
moment the door bursts open, and KING ARNULF enters.

(CONTINUED)

                         KING ARNULF
          Where is he?

                         AUD
          Who, father?

                         KING ARNULF
          Who? Who? Whoever you've got in here,
          of course!

                         AUD
          There *is* no one.

The KING starts prowling around the chamber. ERIK
stands there, naked and petrified, with the cloak
hanging over his head, just where it landed.

                         KING ARNULF
          I can *smell* one of those strangers
          ... That's who it is, isn't it?

AUD keeps mum.

                         KING ARNULF
          This is the fifth one this week.

ERIK gives AUD a look, but she motions him to be
quiet. The KING spins around to see who she is
signaling to.

                         KING ARNULF
          Well, where is he?

The KING appears to be looking straight at ERIK. ERIK
can hardly bear the suspense.

                         AUD
          There's nobody here, father. Look for
          yourself.

KING ARNULF looks around the chamber carefully. He
looks straight through ERIK as if he weren't there.
Suddenly the KING strides over to ERIK and ERIK
instinctively cowers out of the way. The KING walks
straight over to a very small cupboard no more than a
foot high and then flings the door of it open.

                         AUD
          He wouldn't be a midget, father!

                                        (CONTINUED)

The KING turns on her.

> KING ARNULF
> Ah! So you admit there *is* someone!

> AUD
> You're losing your temper!

> KING ARNULF
> (becoming instantly
> pleasant)
> Of course I'm not. I never lose my
> temper ...

ERIK still can't believe that he hasn't been seen.

IVAR's horn sounds again. KING ARNULF looks out of the window and sees Halfdan the Black's ship. A shadow passes over his face.

> KING ARNULF
> Oh, dear ... more visitors!

The KING turns and notices a chest on the floor. He approaches it and knocks on it.

> KING ARNULF
> Come out ... come out like a man ...
> I know you're in there ...

In quite a state the KING flings the chest open, revealing nothing but clothes. He flings the clothes out, and then sits down on the edge – baffled. He casually looks into a trinket box on her table. Nobody in that, either!

> AUD
> (gently)
> It's all in your mind, father ...
> It's you who imagines that I'm always
> up here with some man or other ...

KING ARNULF looks at her and then rises, and walks to the door.

> KING ARNULF
> I don't know how you do it, Aud ... I
> sometimes think you've got some of
> your mother's magic ...

(CONTINUED)

                          AUD
              There is no magic, father ... my
              mother had no magic ...

                          KING ARNULF
              She did, I tell you! She could blind
              me as easily as the night the day.

                          AUD
              It's your fantasy ...

                          KING ARNULF
              But one day I'll catch you ... like I
              caught her ...

He leaves. AUD closes the door. ERIK throws off the
cloak and starts getting dressed.

                          AUD
              The Cloak Invisible. It was my
              mother's parting gift.

                          ERIK
              "The fifth one this week"!

                          AUD
              Oh, for goodness' sake!

                          ERIK
              And I thought you said it was
              something special ...

AUD runs to his side and puts her arms around him.

                          AUD
              That's just what I was trying to tell
              you. You *are* ...

                          ERIK
              Five this week, how many the week
              before?

                          AUD
              You're as bad as my father.

                          ERIK
              And the week before that?

                                        (CONTINUED)

> AUD
> Erik ... !
>> (she is really
>> sincere)
> I want to help you get to Asgaard.

ERIK is torn. He doesn't know whether to believe her
or not. IVAR's horn sounds for a third time. ERIK
races to the window. He looks out. Halfdan's ship is
even closer.

> ERIK

> We mustn't let him land!

> AUD
> Who?

> ERIK
> Halfdan the Black.

> AUD
> But, Erik ...

But ERIK is off out of the door.

> AUD
> No! Wait! My father will be -

There is a thump and a yell off screen.

49 INT.   CORRIDOOR OUTSIDE PRINCESS'S CHAMBER   DAY

ERIK has been set upon by the KING's TWO MUSICIANS.

> KING ARNULF
> I might have known it was you!

> FIRST MUSICIAN
>> (pinning ERIK's arms
>> behind him)
> I'm not hurting you, am I?

> ERIK
> What?

> SECOND MUSICIAN
> You *will* tell us if we hurt you?

(CONTINUED)

They start to march ERIK through the palace.

The horn blows again.

50 INT.   **OUTSIDE THE CELLS   DAY**

> ERIK
> Let me go!

ERIK struggles.

> KING ARNULF
> (to musicians)
> Careful!
> (to ERIK)
> They're not supposed to hurt you.

> ERIK
> You've got to let me go!

> KING ARNULF/OR A MUSICIAN
> Oh no! We can hold on to you - just
> so long as we don't squeeze too hard
> or bump you.

In the distance we hear the horn again.

> ERIK
> Halfdan the Black's here!

51 INT.   **CELL   DAY**

They have reached a cell. The MUSICIANS start to chain
ERIK up.

> KING ARNULF
> It's all part of our safety
> regulations. You see, if someone gets
> hurt they might get angry and then
> ... well ...

> ERIK
> They'll be more than "hurt" if
> Halfdan the Black lands! Ow!

> MUSICIAN
> Ooh! I'm terribly sorry.

(CONTINUED)

KING ARNULF stops them.

                    KING ARNULF
          Who is Halfdan the Black?

                    ERIK
          He's trying to stop us waking the
          Gods.

                    KING ARNULF
          Why?

                    ERIK
          Because that's how he makes his
          money, by war and plunder!

                    KING ARNULF
          Don't talk nonsense.

                    ERIK
          He wants to kill *us*!

                    KING ARNULF
          Not when we explain about the Great
          Blessing.

                    ERIK
          You don't know Halfdan the Black.

                    KING ARNULF
          I know that the Great Blessing has
          kept the peace for a thousand years,
          and will keep it for the next
          thousand.

The horn sounds again. ERIK is about to argue this
point when THORFINN suddenly bursts in.

                    THORFINN
          Erik!

                    MUSICIAN 2
          We're not hurting him.

                    MUSICIAN 1
                    (to ERIK)
          Are we?

                    ERIK
          Just let me go!

                                        (CONTINUED)

> THORFINN
> Halfdan the Black's here!

> ERIK
> I know!

> THORFINN
> (to the king)
> He wants to *kill* us.

They both look at KING ARNULF. The KING thinks.

> ERIK
> You don't want him to kill us *on*
> Hy-Brasil! Do you?

The KING thinks some more. The horn sounds once more.

52 EXT.   GOLDEN DRAGON   SHORE OF HY-BRASIL   DAY

ERIK and the VIKINGS are scrambling into their war
gear. They glance nervously over to where Halfdan the
Black's ship is riding on the waves.

MAGIC MUSIC begins to fill our ears.

ERIK looks around at his men, and then, as if
mesmerized, he moves to the prow and peers out at the
Black Ship, frowning.

THORFINN joins him, followed by IVAR THE BONELESS and
the OTHERS. They all stare out at the black ship.

The MUSIC increases the feelings of magic and tension.

The VIKINGS exchange uneasy glances.

> THORFINN
> I feel strange.

ERIK looks around at THORFINN, shocked.

> IVAR THE BONELESS
> (his throat dry)
> Sort of wobbly and excited?

> THORFINN
> Sort of ...

(CONTINUED)

                         IVAR
          That's fear.

                         ERIK
          But Thorfinn doesn't know the meaning
          of fear.

                         THORFINN
          Is it sort of ... like a sinking
          feeling in your stomach?

                         IVAR
          That's it!

                         ERIK
          But ... you're not even afraid of
          death, Thorfinn!

                         THORFINN
          I know. I know.

                         SVEN'S DAD
          It's magic.

                         ERIK
          What "magic"?

                         SVEN'S DAD
          I've heard stories of a magic that
          strikes fear into the heart so you
          cannot fight.

                         SVEN
                    (deadly serious)
          Yes ... *I* can feel it.

                         IVAR THE BONELESS
                    (eagerly)
          I always feel like this!

HALFDAN'S SHIP starts to move.

                         ERIK
          How does it go so fast?

The OTHERS shake their heads.

ANGLE ON HALFDAN'S SHIP. Suddenly it rises up out of
the water, and reveals the secret of its hidden power.
Under the water line is another line of oars! The

                                        (CONTINUED)

VIKINGS are dumbfounded. IVAR drops trembling to his
knees. The REST go white. THORFINN draws his sword.

ERIK looks around at his MEN with the increasing
realization they are rapidly talking themselves into a
blue funk.

>   ERIK
>   It's not magic! It's just a trick!

>   THORFINN
>   (turning on him
>   angrily)
>   Don't you *feel* it?

ERIK looks around at his paralyzed crew. He realizes
that this is another moment when it is up to him. He
is the only one who can save the situation.

>   ERIK
>   Very well! If they're using magic –
>   we'll us magic of our own!

53 EXT.   OUTSIDE CITY OF HY-BRASIL   DAY

He leaps out of the Golden Dragon and races up to the
shore toward the palace.

54 EXT.   OUTSIDE PALACE OF HY-BRASIL   DAY

ERIK races into the forum and gazes up at the high
walls of the Palace.

>   ERIK
>   Aud! Aud!

There is a slight pause while ERIK tries to make out
which is her room. Eventually AUD puts her head over
the balcony.

>   AUD
>   Sh!

ERIK runs to the wall below her and gazes up. It is a
sheer cliff of crumbling brick and stone, but there
are a couple of protruding gargoyles.

ERIK looks around and sees a MAN tying some things

                                        (CONTINUED)

onto a donkey with a length of rope.

ERIK rushes up to him.

>   ERIK
>   May I?

>   MAN WITH ROPE
>   Of course.

With the aid of the rope, ERIK scales the wall up to
the first gargoyle. Then he produces two knives from
his belt and, in a superb display of gymnastic
ability, ascends the rest of the wall by plunging the
knives into the stonework and hauling himself up, fist
over fist.

When he finally hauls himself into AUD's window there
is a smattering of applause from below. AUD, however,
looks puzzled.

>   AUD
>   Why didn't you come up by the stairs?

ERIK looks around and notices for the first time the
magnificent flights of stairs on either side.

>   ERIK
>   (rather miffed)
>   Just give me a hand.

>   AUD
>   I mean, you could have killed
>   yourself.

>   ERIK
>   Why should *you* care?

>   AUD
>   But I *do*, Erik

ERIK clearly doesn't believe her. He is still
resentful, as she pulls him into the room.

55 INT.   **PRINCESS AUD'S BEDCHAMBER**   **DAY**

ERIK is quite cool with AUD.

>   (CONTINUED)

                         ERIK
             Where's the Cloak Invisible?

                         AUD
       Why?

ERIK looks around and is suddenly suspicious.

                         ERIK
             I can't see it!
                  (indignation
                  suddenly seizes him)
             Have you got another man in ...

ERIK starts feeling the air as if expecting to find an
invisible body.

                         AUD
                  (cutting him off)
         It's in the chest.

ERIK races over and opens it. There is the Cloak.
ERIK's indignation evaporates.

AUD looks at him openly and calmly.

                         AUD
             There won't be "another" man ...

ERIK grunts. He doesn't believe a word of it.

He shrugs and starts toward the window. AUD stops him.

                         AUD
       No!

                         ERIK
             I'll bring it back.

                         AUD
         Erik. You don't understand.

                         ERIK
         No, It's *you* who doesn't understand,
         Aud. Halfdan has come to kill and
         destroy. We brought him here. We must
         stop him.

(CONTINUED)

> AUD
> (pointing at the
> cloak)
> But you don't realize ...

>> ERIK
> Goodbye, Aud ...

ERIK leaps out of the window.

For a moment AUD is surprised and then alarmed as she realizes he's jumped out of the window. We feel she really does care about ERIK.

>> AUD
> Erik!

She rushes to the window in time to see ERIK parachuting down, holding the four corners of the Cloak.

56 EXT. OUTSIDE THE PALACE OF HY-BRASIL DAY

ERIK lands safely and waves the cloak.

>> ERIK
> And thanks for the Cloak Invisible!

>> AUD
> No! WAIT! ERIK! The Cloak! The Cloak
> Invisible! It only seems to work on
> my father!

But ERIK cannot hear her. He is already racing back to his ship.

57 EXT. GOLDEN DRAGON SHORE OF HY-BRASIL DAY

THORFINN is taking "Being Scared" lessons from IVAR THE BONELESS.

>> THORFINN
> And a sort of slightly sick feeling.

>> IVAR
> That's it! *And* you keep wanting to go
> to the lavatory.

(CONTINUED)

> THORFINN
> Oh, yes! I hadn't noticed that!

> SNORRI
> Oh shut up, you two. You're making us
> *all* nervous.

ERIK leaps into Golden Dragon brandishing the Cloak
Invisible.

> ERIK
> So Halfdan the Black's using magic,
> is he? Well, I have here a magic to
> match his!
> > (he holds up the
> > Cloak Invisible)

> KEITEL
> What is it?

> SNORRI
> A magic dishcloth.

> ERIK
> To the oars!

Still in a funk, the VIKINGS take up their places at
the oars. They hang out their shields on the side.
IVAR THE DRUMMER takes his position with his drums.

> THORFINN
> D'you think I've got time to go
> behind that bush?

IVAR starts to drum and the VIKINGS begin to row.

58 EXT. **HALFDAN'S SHIP** **OPEN SEA** **DAY**

ANGLE ON HALFDAN THE BLACK flanked by his ADVISORS,
GISLI ODDSSON and EILIF THE MONGUL. HALFDAN is seated
on a sort of portable throne.

He gives a nod and EILIF bangs his staff of office on
the deck.

The sound of official rapping carries over as we CRANE
DOWN, or CUT into the bowels of the ship.

SLAVES on each side are sweating over their oars. They

58 CONTINUED:

look up and groan with disbelief at the rapping - for
this is the official order to row even faster.

Suddenly the SLAVE-MASTER turns on them. He is a far
from typical slave-master, being a diminutive
Japanese.

He, too has heard the command for a faster rhythm and
he stalks down the decks lashing the sweat-streaked
GALLEY-SLAVES and cursing them in incomprehensible
Japanese.

Fortunately (or perhaps unfortunately) a translation
appears in subtitles.

                    SLAVE-DRIVER
                  (subtitled)
          Row! You incomprehensible,
          horizontal-eyed, Western, trouser
          wetters! Eurgh! You all look the same
          to me! How I despise your lack of
          subtlety and your joined-up writing!
          You, who have never committed ritual
          suicide in your lives!

                    SLAVE
                  (whispering to his
                  neighbor)
          You know, I don't think it would be
          so bad, if we knew what he was
          saying ...

                    SLAVE-DRIVER
          SILENCE! Unceremonious rice-pudding
          eaters! How I abominate your milk
          drinking and your lack of ancestor
          worship and your failure to eat your
          lunch out of little boxes!

59 EXT.   GOLDEN DRAGON   OPEN SEA   DAY

The VIKINGS are rowing. They cannot see the
DOG-SOLDIERS.

                    SVEN'S DAD

          What "magic" have you brought, Erik?

                    ERIK
          You'll see!

60   EXT.   HALFDAN'S SHIP   OPEN SEA   DAY

The prow of the Black Ship turns around so that it is
heading toward Golden Dragon.

Above the shields that line the sides of the ship rise
up FIGURES. They are like the shadows that we glimpsed
back in the courtyard of Halfdan's castle - tall
WARRIORS with spook Dog-Skull helmets.

ANGLE ON HALFDAN and his ADVISORS as HALFDAN gives
another nod, and EILIF raps out yet another command
with his staff.

CLOSE ON the prow of the Black Ship - to see it open
like a pair of jaws.

61   EXT. GOLDEN DRAGON   OPEN SEA   DAY

                        IVAR THE BONELESS
           I've done it!

                        THORFINN
           Oh yes ...
                 (he has too!)

62   EXT.   HALFDAN'S SHIP   OPEN SEA   DAY

ANGLE ON HALFDAN. He nods again and another order is
rapped out.

CLOSE ON the prow. A harpoon is fired. It thuds into
Golden Dragon and appears in front of SNORRI's nose.
Two of HALFDAN's DOG-SOLDIERS start to winch an
attached line in.

63   EXT.   GOLDEN DRAGON   OPEN SEA   DAY

Yells from the VIKINGS as several of them leap to get
the arrows out or to throw sacks over them.

64   EXT.   THE TWO SHIPS   OPEN SEA   DAY

The two ships are hauled closer and closer together by
the lines attached to the harpoons.

                                        (CONTINUED)

64 CONTINUED:

HALFDAN THE BLACK's MEN take their shields off the
side of the ship and rise up, holding their swords
ready to attack.

65 EXT. GOLDEN DRAGON   OPEN SEA   DAY

ERIK's MEN leave their oars and turn to face their
opponents. As they see the strange DOG-SOLDIERS for
the first time, they all go weak at the knees.

But ERIK hastens to reassure them.

He holds up the Cloak Invisible and grins around at
his MEN, knowing he is going to surprise them.

                    ERIK
          Here! Here is magic from the King's
          Daughter.

ERIK enjoys the moment of suspense. Then he throws the
Cloak Invisible over his head and shoulders and grins
around at his MEN triumphantly, imagining that he has
vanished from their sight.

                    ERIK
          I have become the wind!

The VIKINGS look at him rather puzzled.

66 EXT.   SEA BATTLE   DAY

Suddenly the Black Ship scrapes up against the Golden
Dragon. SNORRI tries to push them apart.

ERIK, however, leaps onto the side of Golden Dragon,
and nimbly runs along the edge to the prow and stands
there still imagining he is invisible.

                    HARALD THE MISSIONARY
          How did he do that?

                    SVEN'S DAD
          What?

                    HARALD THE MISSIONARY
          Vanish into thin air.

                                        (CONTINUED)

                         SVEN'S DAD
          He hasn't.

                         HARALD THE MISSIONARY
          Well, where is he?

HARALD looks around. He is the only one who can't see
ERIK.

                         SVEN'S DAD
          He's there!

HALFDAN's MEN are a bit nonplussed (as indeed are
ERIK's) as ERIK runs along the side of the ship.

Suddenly ERIK leaps from one ship to the other. He
runs through ONE MAN and then ANOTHER. Then he starts
jumping up and down on the prow of HALFDAN's ship
pulling faces.

                         ERIK
          Boooo! You can't see me! But I can
          see you!

He grimaces at HALFDAN's MEN, skips to one side and
then attacks. HALFDAN's MEN are totally unnerved by
this fearless behavior.

ANGLE ON HALFDAN looking disturbed. His face seems
more sinister than before.

                         HALFDAN
          What's going on?

                         GISLI ODDSSON
          That's Erik.

                         HALFDAN
          Well, why isn't he scared of us?

ANGLE ON ERIK.

                         ERIK
          What's it like to feel the wind? Eh?
                  (he runs another
                  through)
          Sharp, isn't it?

ERIK leaps onto the side of the ship and does his
balancing act, running along it to the other end of

                                          (CONTINUED)

the ship. Then he jumps up and down.

> ERIK
> Look! Look! Here I am! Ha ha!

ONE DOG-SOLDIER looks at ANOTHER in total
incomprehension of this unwarranted behavior. ERIK
takes the chance to push him over the edge.

The DOG-SOLDIER topples over into the hold amongst the
wretched GALLEY-SLAVES who look at each other and then
back up to ERIK to witness him running through yet
another dumb-struck DOG-SOLDIER. The toppled
DOG-SOLDIER has been knocked out by his fall.

The GALLEY-SLAVES take heart from ERIK's example and
ONE of them throws down his oar, picks up the
DOG-SOLDIER's sword and runs him through.

> SLAVE-MASTER
> (subtitled)
> Hey! What's going on? Your
> big-breasted women give me no
> pleasure with their warmed-up fish
> and ... urgh!

The SLAVE-MASTER strides down the ship to flay the
offending SLAVE, but ANOTHER trips him up and in a
twinkling of an eye FOUR OTHERS have leapt on the
SLAVE-MASTER (despite their chains) and are extracting
his keys.

CUT TO:

HALFDAN, who is screaming at his nonplussed
DOG-SOLDIERS.

> HALFDAN
> What's the matter? Haven't you seen
> anyone fight before?

> DOG-SOLDIER
> No.

> ANOTHER
> They're usually too scared.

> HALFDAN
> *Kill* him!

(CONTINUED)

Back on board Golden Dragon, the VIKINGS look at each
other in admiration. Even KEITEL.

SVEN'S DAD nudges his SON.

> SVEN'S DAD
> There! *That's* a true Berserk!

> SVEN
> I'm just building up to it, Dad.

SVEN starts banging his head on the side of the boat.

> SNORRI
> He's gone batty!

> THORFINN
> No! The fear's gone!

THORFINN screams and charges, followed by SVEN'S DAD.

> CUT TO:

ERIK wreaking havoc amongst the stunned DOG-SOLDIERS
who are now only just beginning to fight back.

ANGLE ON HALFDAN, jumping up and down on his throne.

> HALFDAN
> (the evilness
> showing for the
> first time)
> Fight, damn you! Fight!

> HALFDAN grabs a sword off one of his
> dead DOG-SOLDIERS and starts to join
> in.

ANGLE ON the Golden Dragon.

The rest of the MEN are leaping into action - except
KEITEL and HARALD THE MISSIONARY. SNORRI looks back at
KEITEL.

> SNORRI
> Well! Come on!

> KEITEL
> I ... I ...

> (CONTINUED)

KEITEL is thinking: "Maybe I should let Halfdan win" but knows he can't let a thing like that happen, now that he is faced with the reality of it. The companionship of the voyage has brought them all too close for that. HARALD gives him a curious look. At this moment, KEITEL notices ERIK fighting a DOG-SOLDIER, whom IVAR THE BONELESS is beating over the head with his drumsticks. Suddenly IVAR is run through from behind, and a second DOG-SOLDIER joins the attack on ERIK.

> KEITEL
> Hang the Blacksmith's Code!

KEITEL leaps to his feet and joins in the attack. His sword slices through everything.

> CUT TO:

ERIK fighting as if he were invisible, swinging across the deck on a rope.

> ERIK
> I am the air! I am the wind!

Fighting side by side with the OTHERS, KEITEL begins to feel the camaraderie.

THORFINN grins across at him.

> THORFINN
> This is the life, eh?

KEITEL grins and strikes out.

SVEN and his DAD are fighting alongside each other.

> SVEN'S DAD
> Well, go on! Go berserk!

> SVEN
> GIVE US A CHANCE, Dad!

> SNORRI
> (to SVEN'S DAD)
> What about you? Why don't *you* go berserk?

> SVEN'S DAD
> I got to keep my eye on *him* ...

> (CONTINUED)

                        SVEN
              Look out! Thorfinn!

Suddenly THORFINN is run through. SVEN goes berserk
and kills the DOG-SOLDIER who did it. Then he charges
off totally berserk. No one can stand in his way.

SVEN'S DAD looks proud.

                                        CUT TO:

More and more GALLEY-SLAVES swarming onto the deck and
overwhelming the DOG-SOLDIERS with swords and oars.

Sequence of DOG-SOLDIERS being thrown over the side or
killed.

The DOG-SOLDIERS are totally overwhelmed by the
numbers.

                                        CUT TO:

HALFDAN and his ADVISORS slipping into a lifeboat and
sneaking off. The rats leave the sinking ship.

                                        CUT TO:

ERIK about to run a DOG-SOLDIER through.

                        DOG-SOLDIER
              No! No! Wait!

ERIK hesitates. KEITEL exchanges glances with ERIK, as
the DOG-SOLDIER puts his fingers to his neck and
apparently rips off his face to reveal it was a mask
and that he is, in fact, LOKI.

ERIK is totally nonplussed. KEITEL is immediately
amazed and guilt-stricken at the same time.

                        ERIK
              LOKI!

Meanwhile the DOG-SOLDIERS are all killed, and the
GALLEY-SLAVES are cheering their victory. VIKINGS and
GALLEY-SLAVES are hugging each other.

                        ERIK
              Where did *you* come from?

                                        (CONTINUED)
                        101

                              LOKI
                         (to Erik)
                    Halfdan wanted to stop you waking the
                    Gods ... so ...
                              (he glances across
                              at Keitel)
                    So ... I disguised myself ... to
                    sabotage his plans.

The VIKINGS look around in disbelief.

ERIK is about to say "But it was the magic cloak":

                              ERIK
          But −

                              LOKI
                    It was my master Keitel's idea.

All eyes turn on KEITEL who looks very uncomfortable.

                              LOKI
                    Wasn't it, Keitel?

                              KEITEL
                    Well ... I ... I ... thought ...

KEITEL is overcome by the power of LOKI's will, but he
is deeply ashamed of his complicity in LOKI's deeds.
SNORRI gazes at KEITEL with deep suspicion.

                                                  CUT TO:

SVEN. He is cradling the dying THORFINN in his arms.

                              SVEN
                    Thorfinn! You can't die!

                              THORFINN
                    I'm not frightened ... of anything ...

                              SVEN
                    You'll see my grandfather in
                    Valhalla!

                              THORFINN
                         (dying)
                    No ... he's not ... not ...

                                            (CONTINUED)

                              SVEN
                    Tell him I'm coming!

THORFINN dies. SVEN holds him and a tear comes down
his face. The danger has made comrades of the two
rivals.

They all look at ERIK. ERIK looks back at them.

                              ERIK
                    But ... how is it you can see me?
                              (he looks around)
                    You can all see me?

                              LOKI
                    What d'you mean?

                              SNORRI AND OTHERS
                    Why shouldn't we see you?

                              HARALD
                    I can't see him.

                              ERIK
                    I'm wearing the Cloak Invisible ...

ERIK takes it off to demonstrate.

                              HARALD THE MISSIONARY
                    Oh! There you are!

                              ERIK
                              (to the others)
                    You mean ... you could see me all the
                    time?

The VIKINGS look at each other mystified.

                              SNORRI
                    Weren't we supposed to?

                              ERIK
                    Oh ... I feel a little ... oh ...

ERIK's knees give way and he faints onto the deck.

67 INT.   THE KING'S HALL   HY-BRASIL   DAY

KING ARNULF is thanking ERIK and his MEN for saving

                                        (CONTINUED)

them. AUD looks across at ERIK and smiles, hoping he
will return it. He does not.

> KING ARNULF
> We are grateful to you, Erik, and
> your men ...

> COURT
> Yes, we are ...

> KING ARNULF
> And there is only *one* way we can
> repay you ...

KING ARNULF claps his hands. Two MUSICIANS hurry out.

> ERIK
> (hurriedly)
> Well, we'd love to hear you sing
> again, but what we'd really
> appreciate would be if you could see
> your way to lending ... not giving,
> of course ...

All the time ERIK is talking, the doors of the hall
behind are opening and a vast LUR or HORN is being
brought in carried by SIX BEARERS. One or two of the
VIKINGS have turned to look and are now standing
speechless.

ERIK, however, is intent on his plea to the KING.

> ERIK
> (continuing)
> ... but just lending us the ... um
> ... the, well to be quite blunt ...
> the Horn Resounding.

KING ARNULF beams at ERIK. Now ERIK finally turns and
looks at what everybody else is looking at.

ERIK jaw drops.

> KING ARNULF
> (beaming)
> It's yours.

Everyone in the court beams at ERIK, except AUD who is
looking sad and disappointed.

(CONTINUED)

> ERIK
> (when he can find
> his voice)
> Is *that* it?

A cloud passes over KING ARNULF's face.

> KING ARNULF
> Is there something the matter with
> it?

> ERIK
> Oh! No! No ... of course not ... it's
> just I hadn't expected it to be quite
> so big.

> KING ARNULF
> Well, it's not called the Horn
> Resounding for nothing.
> (aside)
> You *do* know how to play the Horn,
> don't you?

> ERIK
> Yes ... oh, yes ...

> KING ARNULF
> Then I expect you'll be leaving first
> thing in the morning.

AUD tries to catch ERIK's eye, but he avoids her. AUD
looks miserable as the KING manhandles her away.

68 INT.   THE KING'S HALL   HY-BRASIL   NIGHT

The CAMERA PANS over the sleeping forms of the other
VIKINGS, lying in the Great Hall beside the Horn
Resounding, which glows in the darkness.

The CAMERA CLOSES in on KEITEL. TENSE MUSIC starts to
play. Suddenly a VOICE comes from the shadows:

> VOICE
> (whispering)
> Keitel! Keitel Blacksmith!

KEITEL opens his eyes and finds LOKI close beside him.

(CONTINUED)

> LOKI
> What's the matter, Keitel Blacksmith?
> Have you forgotten why you came on
> this voyage?

KEITEL is silent.

> LOKI
> Are you going to let ERIK wake the
> Gods?

> KEITEL
> How can we stop him now?

LOKI looks around and then opens his hand in front of
KEITEL. In it is the mouthpiece from the Horn
Resounding. It glows in the darkness.

> LOKI
> Take this and throw it from the cliff
> heights. They'll never make the Horn
> Resounding sound without it.

KEITEL grins. Then an obvious thought limps across his
muscular mind.

> KEITEL
> But why me? Why don't you do it?

SOMEBODY stirs.

> LOKI
> Sh! Hurry!

> KEITEL
> *You* do it!

> LOKI
> You'll be able to throw it further
> than I could.

KEITEL thinks. This is true.

> LOKI
> It must go far out to sea.

LOKI presses the mouthpiece on KEITEL. KEITEL takes
it, but reluctantly. ANOTHER VIKING stirs.

(CONTINUED)

                          LOKI
              Surely you haven't forgotten your
              Blacksmith's Oath?

KEITEL is about to reply and say he's been having
second thoughts about it, but somehow he can't. LOKI
has such power over him.

                          KEITEL
              I ...

Suddenly ANOTHER VIKING stirs, and LOKI hisses at him.

                          LOKI
              Hurry!

LOKI pretends to go back to sleep. KEITEL (feeling a
bit lumbered) thinks about his task and hesitates ...
who knows? Perhaps he is about to stand firm, but LOKI
plays his trump card.

                          LOKI
                    (without opening his
                    eyes)
              Or I might have to tell Erik why you
              really came on this voyage.

KEITEL is caught. He closes his eyes in resignation
and then reluctantly starts to make his way out of the
Hall.

As he gets to the doors he trips over SNORRI, who
wakes. The mouthpiece falls a few feet away.

                          SNORRI
              Who's that!

                          KEITEL
              It's me. I'm just going to water the
              dragon ...
                    (he gives a false
                    laugh)

                          SNORRI
              Oh ...

SNORRI notices the silver mouthpiece on the floor, but
he pretends he hasn't.

                                        (CONTINUED)

> SNORRI
> Oh ... clumsy idiot.

SNORRI pretends to go back to sleep, but he opens one eye and watches KEITEL BLACKSMITH recover the mouthpiece, and then follows KEITEL out.

LOKI gets up, too. He follows to keep an eye on SNORRI.

69 EXT.   CLIFF-TOP   HY-BRASIL   DAWN

ANGLE ON AUD sitting under some cliffs, gazing moodily out to sea. She is brooding on ERIK's imminent departure.

Suddenly a stone falls from above, and she looks up and sees a FIGURE appear on the cliff above. Huriedly she withdraws into the shadows.

The CAMERA PANS up to KEITEL BLACKSMITH standing on the cliff-top. In his hands he holds the mouthpiece of the Horn Resounding. He examines it, turning over in his mind whether he is doing the right thing or not. Then he decides he must.

> KEITEL
> (to himself)
> My fellow blacksmiths.

He prepares to throw it.

> SNORRI (V.O.)
> Keitel!

KEITEL jumps out of his skin.

> KEITEL
> What?

> SNORRI
> What are you doing, Keitel Blacksmith?

> KEITEL
> Get away, Snorri.

> SNORRI
> What have you got there?

(CONTINUED)

SNORRI advances toward KEITEL. KEITEL backs away,
dangerously near to the edge of the cliff. His boot
slips and he jerks himself forward. At the same time
SNORRI makes a grab for the mouthpiece.

A violent scuffle ensues.

CUT TO:

LOKI watching from a hiding place. From his jerkin he
produces a knife. The blade glints in the first rays
of the sun.

CUT TO:

SNORRI and KEITEL locked in mortal combat. In the
middle of it all, the mouthpiece of the Horn
Resounding is dropped.

The CAMERA follows the mouthpiece as it bounces off
the cliff and falls down to the shore below.

AUD steps out of the shadow and picks it up. She
frowns and looks up, and then screams.

AUD
No!

Meanwhile, KEITEL is in danger of being pushed over
the edge. Suddenly, however, SNORRI goes white and
gives a hideous gasp ... his eyes staring, he turns to
find LOKI standing with a bloody knife, and he
realizes his back is covered in his own blood. He
can't make a sound, however, and he sinks slowly to
his knees.

As KEITEL and LOKI watch him die, a drop of blood from
the knife drops (in slow motion) to the ground. The
moment it does there is a deep, subterranean groan,
and the earth begins to tremble violently.

KEITEL and LOKI look around in alarm.

KEITEL
Oh, Gods! What have we done?

70 INT.   THE KING'S HALL   HY-BRASIL   DAY

ERIK, SVEN, SVEN'S DAD and HARALD are wide awake, but

(CONTINUED)

for the moment paralyzed – unsure whether to run or wait for the earthquake to stop, as bits of masonry crash around them.

Suddenly KING ARNULF appears at the top of a stairway. He raises his hands.

> KING ARNULF
> Stay calm! This is *not* happening.

The KING then hurries out of a door at the top of the staircase.

> SVEN'S DAD
> What did he say?

Suddenly the building gives an extra violent shudder and a huge cornice crashes to the ground, almost braining one of the VIKINGS.

> ERIK
> Look out!

The doors of the Great Hall burst open and a wall of water crashes through, knocking the VIKINGS off their feet.

71 INT.   THE FORUM   HY-BRASIL   DAY

KING ARNULF is standing at the top of the Forum steps addressing a crowd of anxious CITIZENS. They are keeping surprisingly good order considering they are already standing ankle-deep in water, and the whole town is rapidly sinking around them.

> KING ARNULF
> Now, I know what some of you must be
> thinking ... the day has come ...
> we're all going down etc. etc. But
> let's get away from the fantasy and
> look at the *FACTS*.
> *FACT (1)* The threat of total
> destruction has kept the peace for
> one thousand years.
> *FACT (2)* The chances of it failing
> now are therefore 1 in 365,000.
> *FACT (3)* ...

(CONTINUED)

By this time the water is up to the CITIZENS' knees,
and SEVERAL have crowded onto the lower steps to avoid
getting wet.

> KING ARNULF
> *FACT (3)* Our safety regulations are
> the most rigorous in the world. We
> are all nice to each other, we never
> rub each other the wrong way or
> contradict each other, do we?

> CROWD
> No.

RUMBLE. The building sinks and masonry falls.

> CITIZEN
> We ... er ... do seem to be going
> down quite fast, your Majesty – not
> trying to contradict you, of course.

> KING ARNULF
> No, of course you're not, citizen.
> But let's stick to the facts. There
> has *never* been a safer, more certain
> way of keeping the peace. So
> whatever's happening, you can rest
> assured, Hy-Brasil is *not* sinking.
> Repeat, *not* sinking.

The CITIZENS seem reasonably reassured by this – even
though many of them are now up to their waists. More
RUMBLES and crashing masonry.

> ANOTHER CITIZEN
> May I just make a point in support of
> what King Arnulf's just said?

> KING ARNULF
> We'd be delighted – wouldn't we?

> CITIZENS
> Yes, we'd certainly like to hear what
> one of us has got to say ...

ERIK, SVEN, SVEN'S DAD and HARALD struggle out of the
Great Hall, carrying their belongings and the Horn
Resounding while the CITIZEN is still speaking most
articulately in support of the KING. They are *almost*
in panic.

(CONTINUED)

> ERIK
> What are you all doing?

> CITIZEN AT THE BACK
> (cheerfully)
> It's all right. It's not happening.

> ERIK
> (urgently)
> The place is sinking!

> CITIZEN AT THE BACK
> Yes, I thought it was, too, but the
> King's just pointed out that it can't
> be.

> CITIZEN
> (still speaking in
> support of the King)
> ... and, of course, we mustn't forget
> King Arnulf's *excellent* eye for
> flower-arranging.

A smattering of applause. A FEW PEOPLE pull their
robes up out of the wet.

ERIK leaps onto a wall and shouts to the CROWD. He is
almost beside himself between his sense of urgency and
his amazement at the obtuseness of the Hy-Brasilians.

> ERIK
> Save yourselves! Hy-Brasil ... is
> sinking!

RUMBLES and more sinking.

There are a lot of knowing smiles amongst the
CITIZENS.

> CITIZEN FROM MIDDLE
> Look, you don't know our safety
> regulations.

> KING ARNULF
> It can't happen.

> ERIK
> But it *is*! Look!

(CONTINUED)

112

                         KING ARNULF
                        (ignoring ERIK)
              The important thing is not to panic.

                          CITIZENS
              Quite ... yes ... we understand ...

                         KING ARNULF
              I've already appointed the Chancellor
              as the Chairman of a committee to
              find out exactly what *is* going on,
              and meantime I suggest we have a
              sing-song!

                          CITIZENS
              Good idea!

                          ANOTHER
              Can we do the one that goes "TUM-TI-
              TUM-TI-TUM-TI-TUM"?

ERIK looks around in despair and then nods to his MEN.

72 **EXT.   A FLOODED STREET   DAY**

The terrible noise of a "sing-song" starts up as we
CUT AWAY to another street. The street promptly sinks
up to roof level, and we hear sudden screaming: "Help!
Help!"

We MOVE IN closer to see from under a canopy two
struggling FIGURES emerge. They are LOKI and KEITEL.

LOKI is thrashing about in a panic and KEITEL is
trying to control him.

                          LOKI
              I can't swim! I can't swim!

                          KEITEL
              Relax!

                          LOKI
              I'm drowning! Help!

LOKI grabs KEITEL around the neck.

                          KEITEL
              Let go!

                                        (CONTINUED)

                            113

But KEITEL is pulled under. He re-emerges spluttering.

> KEITEL
>> Urrgh! Argh! Let go, you idiot!

> LOKI
>> Help!

> KEITEL
>> You'll drown us bo... !

But they go under again.

> CUT TO:

The other end of the street, as ERIK, SVEN, SVEN'S DAD and HARALD swim around the corner pushing the Horn Resounding, which floats on its wooden base.

They see FIGURES disappearing under the water.

KEITEL and LOKI reappear for a moment.

> KEITEL
>> Help!

> LOKI
>> Help!

ERIK, SVEN and CO. swim as fast as they can to rescue the drowning PAIR. They struggle to overpower the panic-stricken LOKI, but he puts up a manic fight.

Unexpectedly, HARALD THE MISSIONARY suddenly unleashes a vicious right hook and lays LOKI out cold.

There is a moment's stunned silence that is not unmingled with indignation.

> SVEN
>> (with hurt surprise)
>> You hit him!

> HARALD
>> Well, it's what you're supposed to do ... isn't it?

> SVEN'S DAD
>> Look!

(CONTINUED)

They look up and MAGIC MUSIC fills the air as GOLDEN
DRAGON sails around a corner of the street.

The VIKINGS haul the still unconscious LOKI onto the
roof of the canopy and their SHIP draws up alongside
them.

Suddenly ERIK catches sight of AUD at the helm and for
a moment his joy seems stalled.

>   ERIK
>   Oh ... it's you!

>   AUD
>   Where's my father?

>   ERIK
>   But how did you ... ?

Suddenly the "sing-song" reaches a particularly noisy
and discordant climax. They all turn.

>   AUD
>   Quick!

73 EXT.   THE FORUM TEMPLE ROOF   DAY

ANGLE ON the Forum. The only building left is the roof
of the Forum Temple. A crowd of unconcerned CITIZENS
is sitting on the roof and just coming to the end of
another appalling song.

>   CITIZENS
>   ... Te ... Tum!

>   KING ARNULF
>   You know, I think we're getting
>   better.

>   CITIZEN 1
>   (with genuine
>   interest)
>   How can you tell?

>   KING ARNULF
>   Er ...

(CONTINUED)

>   AUD
>   Father!

The KING looks up.

>   KING ARNULF
>   It's all right! It isn't happening!

>   AUD
>   But, father, it *is*!

>   ERIK
>   Get on board!

>   CITIZEN 2
>   No *thanks*!

>   CITIZEN 3
>   Who do you think *you* are?

>   CITIZEN 1
>   Panic-monger!

KEITEL is trying to haul one CITIZEN aboard. the CITIZEN fights him off.

>   CITIZEN
>   Leave us alone!

>   SVEN
>   Yeah, leave 'em alone.

>   AUD
>   It's sinking! Hy-Brasil is sinking!

>   KING ARNULF
>   Well, my dear, I think you'll find
>   it's all a question of what you want
>   to believe in ... I have slightly
>   more experience of these matters than
>   you ...

Unfortunately, at this point, the entire gathering of CITIZENS, the KING, and the Forum Temple disappear below the waves.

>   AUD
>   Father!
>   (tears spring to her
>   eyes)

(CONTINUED)

HARALD THE MISSIONARY has put his arm around AUD in a
fatherly way.

                    HARALD THE MISSIONARY
               There, my child ... it's at times
               like this that this book can be a
               great help ...

ERIK shoos him away.

                    HARALD THE MISSIONARY
                         (with his usual
                         promptness)
          Right.

74 EXT.   SEA AND MOUNTAINS   DAY

LONG SHOT of Golden Dragon.

In the distance a range of mountains sinks beneath the
water.

Golden Dragon spins alone in the wide ocean.

                                             FADE.

75 EXT.   GOLDEN DRAGON - OPEN SEA   DAY

A big CLOSE-UP of ERIK.

                         ERIK
                    (to himself)
               We must blow the first note ... the
               note that will take us to Asgaard ...

                         SVEN
                    (nervously and with
                    awe in his voice)
               Over the Edge of the World.

                         LOKI
                    (even more
                    nervously)
               Wouldn't it be better to go home now?

The other MEN look up at the Horn Resounding, and
begin to feel a bit nervous.

                                        (CONTINUED)

SINISTER MUSIC.

>   ERIK
>   We are going where only the dead have
>   been before ...

ERIK takes a deep breath and then puts his lips to the
Horn Resounding. He blows. There is a splutter, and
one or two of the VIKINGS titter amongst themselves.

He has another go. But again, all he produces is a
pathetic spluttering.

>   SVEN
>   (not unkindly in his
>   manner)
>   Uh! Here! Give it to me!

SVEN pushes ERIK aside.

SVEN blows ... he becomes redder and redder. But all
he produces is a splutter. He gets a bit angry.

>   SVEN
>   Damn it!

SVEN'S DAD looks heavenward.

>   SVEN'S DAD
>   You're not using the right technique.

SVEN'S DAD tries to take it over but SVEN won't let
him.

>   SVEN
>   No! I'm doing it!

They start to struggle.

>   SVEN
>   (getting angry)
>   You're always telling me ... *telling*
>   me!

ERIK tries to separate them.

>   ERIK
>   Sven!

(CONTINUED)

>   SVEN
>   (to his Dad)
>   Let me do something for myself for a
>   change!

ANGLE ON AUD. She is at the back of the boat weeping
and being comforted by HARALD. Nevertheless, she looks
up.

>   AUD
>   No! Don't quarrel!

SVEN and HIS DAD stop fighting, surprised by the
vehemence in her voice.

AUD picks herself up and crosses over to them,
brushing away her tears.

>   AUD
>   We'll never get where we want to go
>   if we fight.

The VIKINGS stand in front of AUD like naughty
schoolboys.

>   SVEN
>   Sorry.

>   SVEN'S DAD
>   Sorry.

>   ERIK
>   We?

AUD crosses to the HORN and inserts the mouthpiece.
She looks at the Horn.

>   AUD
>   It has not spoken for a thousand
>   years ... you must bring it to life
>   with a kiss ...

She puts her lips to the mouthpiece and just touches
it with them ... almost a kiss ... then ... very
gently ... she begins to blow ... a soft ... slight
note can be heard ...

AUD takes her mouth away from the mouthpiece ... and
the soft note goes on ... reverberating ... a sweet
note ... a magic note ... the VIKINGS stand stock

                                        (CONTINUED)

still, enchanted by the sound ... and the sound all
the time is getting louder and the Horn begins to
vibrate with the note. As the volume increases the
Golden Dragon itself begins to reverberate with the
sound. Rings of ripples begin to radiate out from the
boat across the calm water. As the note gets louder,
the film seems to go into stereo for the first time
and the sound is all around.

The note gets louder and louder, and the VIKINGS, who
at first were laughing and cheering AUD's success,
begin to get rather alarmed.

Louder and louder gets the note and the Horn shakes
and the boat vibrates. Things start to be shaken loose
and fall onto the deck. Ropes uncoil and run loose.

>   ERIK
>   Look out!

But he's too late. The spar suddenly crashes down to
the deck, crowning HARALD and laying him out flat.

LOUDER and LOUDER grows the note, and the VIKINGS have
to stop their ears for the pain. Pegs are shaken loose
and fall to the deck. The mast itself crashes down on
them. The water around the ship becomes more and more
agitated.

And then another sound is heard. It is the thunder of
water in the distance like a million distant
waterfalls.

And suddenly they notice the sea is running like a
river - all in one direction ... sweeping the ship
forward with incredible momentum.

76 **EXT.   SEA-MIST   BEFORE THE EDGE OF THE WORLD   DAY**

... and they are engulfed in a mist, still travelling
at a rate of knots.

Almost at once a pointed rock looms out of the mist
ahead of them.

ERIK flings himself at the steering oar, and EVERYONE
is thrown about as the ship veers wildly and just
misses the rock, only to see another looming up ahead

                                        (CONTINUED)

of them. The ship veers again, as a third rock looms
ahead.

This time SVEN has grabbed a coil of rope, and as they
pass the third rock, he throws it like a lasso over
the rock. LOKI and KEITEL grasp the rope as well.

                    LOKI
          Help!

The OTHERS leap to grab the rope just as the rope goes
taut and the ship comes to a lurching stop, anchored
by the rope, but still swaying and buffeted in the
racing waters.

Those on board shout to each other, soaked to the
skin. It is difficult to make out what they are
shouting.

AUD touches the Horn Resounding and it stops. Or maybe
it just dies away.

                    AUD
               (shouting to Loki)
          What are you doing?

                    LOKI
          What d'you think? Help! Somebody help
          us!

                    SVEN
          Shut up!

                    LOKI
               (pointing at Aud)
          She wants to kill us!

                    KEITEL
          She wants to take us over the Edge of
          the World!

                    AUD
          You want to get to Asgaard, don't
          you?

                    LOKI
               (pointing an
               accusing finger at
               AUD)
          How do we know this is the way?

                                        (CONTINUED)

ERIK, alomost despite himself, finds himself coming to
AUD's defense.

>   ERIK
>   (shouting)
> We blew the Horn Resounding.

>   LOKI
>   (shouting)
> *She* blew the Horn Resounding.

>   KEITEL
>   (shouting)
> Don't you see, Erik? She wants
> revenge!

ERIK glances uncomfortably at AUD - he still doesn't
totally trust her.

>   ERIK
> What are you talking about?

>   LOKI
>   (to KEITEL)
> Shut up!

>   KEITEL
> She knows it was our fault!

>   LOKI
> Keep your mouth shut, Keitel!

>   KEITEL
> No! It's *you*, Loki! I never should
> have listened to you!

LOKI looks around desperately.

>   LOKI
> You've lost your mind.

>   KEITEL
> We came to stop you waking the Gods,
> Erik. But I didn't want anyone to get
> hurt!

>   LOKI
> You fool!

LOKI leaps on KEITEL and tries to stab him.

(CONTINUED)

> > > LOKI
> > I should have got rid of you long
> > ago!

> > > KEITEL
> > Like you got rid of Snorri!

ERIK grabs LOKI's hand that holds the knife.

> > > AUD
> > No! No! We are in the spell of the
> > Horn! Hatred will destroy us!

> > > ERIK
> > That's right!

For a split second ERIK is distracted. He looks across
at AUD and for a moment he sees FREYA standing there.

> > > FREYA
> > Once you are in the spell of the
> > Horn, hatred will destroy you ...

Then it is AUD once more. But in that split second
LOKI has stabbed ERIK's arm.

> > > ERIK
> > Arrgh!

ERIK staggers back, bleeding.

KEITEL gives a roar of rage, and picks LOKI up bodily
and hurls him off of the boat into the maelstrom.

The other VIKINGS look on aghast. KEITEL turns on
them.

> > > KEITEL
> > He killed Snorri! He caused the land
> > of Hy-Brasil to sink! *She* knew!

> > > AUD
> > I didn't know!

> > > KEITEL
> > Now she wants to send us over the
> > Edge of the World!

(CONTINUED)

> AUD
>
> How else d'you think we're going to
> get to Asgaard?

The VIKINGS look at each other amidst the roaring
waters and the thick spray. ERIK holds his bleeding
arm and looks at AUD. He doen't know what to think
about her. Should he trust her or not?

AUD looks at him in mute appeal. ERIK avoids her gaze
and turns to the OTHERS.

> ERIK
> (shouting above the
> din)
> Do *you* know the way to Asgaard,
> Keitel Blacksmith?

KEITEL shakes his head.

> ERIK
> Do *you* know the way to Asgaard, Sven?

SVEN shakes his head.

> ERIK
> There is only one road before us, and
> that leads over the Edge of the
> World.

ANGLE ON HARALD - still unconscious, but he murmers in
his unconsciousness:

> HARALD
> There *is* no Edge of the World.

SVEN'S DAD (who has been reviving him) bonks him
again.

ERIK takes the rope and begins paying it out.

With grim faces the VIKINGS turn and face toward the
roaring of the waters, as ERIK edges the ship further
into the mist.

ANGLE ON GOLDEN DRAGON disappearing into the spray
again.

ANGLE ON the VIKINGS in the midst of the spray. The
noise is deafening. It would be almost impossible to

(CONTINUED)

hear any voice above it.

The VIKINGS pass through the SHOT - and disappear
again into the mist.

QUICK CLOSE-UPS of the VIKINGS' faces. ERIK ... KEITEL
... SVEN ... SVEN'S DAD ... then AUD - looking just as
frightened as the rest of them ...

                                        CUT TO:

The VIKINGS' POINT OF VIEW. The prow of the Golden
Dragon emerges out of the spray-mist.

77 EXT.   THE EDGE OF THE WORLD   DAY

WONDROUS MUSIC as we emerge to see the Waterfall of
the Seas - stretching on either side of us - as far as
the eye can see - water falling and plunging over the
lip of the world. And in front of us - the blue sky
continues on down and down until it shades into
blackness strewn with stars beneath our feet ...

SVEN, SVEN'S DAD and KEITEL edge to the prow and gasp.

ERIK, at the back of the ship, pays out a little more
line. The ship inches forward.

                                        CUT TO:

A view of the Waterfall of Seas with the ship edging
toward the rim.

                    AUD
            No! Don't look over the Edge!

They let out a little more, until the ship is
protruding over the edge.

SHOT from below of SVEN, SVEN'S DAD, and KEITEL
peering over the side, looking down into the abyss and
gasping.

                                        CUT TO:

A SHOT from above. We see the prow of Golden Dragon
and the backs of the VIKING's HEADS in plain view
against a backdrop of stars below them.

                                    (CONTINUED)

CUT TO:

The stern of the longship.

>   AUD
>   Don't!

>   ERIK
>   (shouting above the
>   noise)
>   What can you see?

CUT TO:

The VIKINGS at the prow, looking over the edge (shot from below). They are speechless.

>   SVEN'S DAD
>   Oh ... Gods ...

As they gaze down into the bottomless chasm where the clear blue sky turns to night – an under-sky full of stars, their heads begin to spin.

>   SVEN'S DAD
>   Nothing ... we are nothing ...

>   SVEN
>   I feel so peaceful ...

A calmness seems to have settled over them.

>   ERIK
>   What can you see?

KEITEL turns.

>   KEITEL
>   Eternity. You have taken us to the
>   Edge of Eternity.

>   ERIK
>   Let me see!

AUD holds him back.

>   AUD
>   No. don't look ... the abyss will
>   suck away your strength.

(CONTINUED)

                              ERIK
              I *must* look! Keitel! Hold this!

ERIK turns to see SVEN and KEITEL trembling ... they
hold on to the sides of the ship but their legs can
barely support them.

                              SVEN
              There is nothing we can do ...

                         SVEN'S DAD
                Helpless ...

KEITEL starts to laugh.

                             KEITEL
              Ha ha ... I believed Loki ... I
              believed I had a duty to blacksmiths!
              Ha ha ha!

KEITEL laughs a little hysterically.

                              ERIK
                Keitel!

                              AUD
              Erik! You must decide!

                              ERIK
                           (to AUD)
              But what do they see?

                              AUD
              Will you trust me?

ERIK turns and looks at AUD. Does he trust her?

                              AUD
              You still want to get to Asgaard?

                              ERIK
                Of course.

                              AUD
              Do you believe I love you?

                              ERIK
              I ... but I ...

                                        (CONTINUED)

> > AUD
> > You don't have to love me. Just: Do
> > you believe *I* love *you*?
>
> > ERIK
> > Yes - I believe you do.
>
> > AUD
> > Then let go!

ERIK hesitates, then he decides to believe in AUD. He
throws the rope away.

The ship shoots off the Edge of the World into SPACE ...

78 EXT.   SKY AND WATERFALL   DAY

Everthing seems to slow down as the longship drops
down and down ... the ship twists slowly as it drops
... around and around.

The VIKINGS gaze about them in wonder.

79 EXT.   SPACE   DAY

Gradually the sky fades to black .. until the ship is
falling in silence amongst the stars.

HARALD comes to once again.

> > HARALD
> > I'm still seeing stars.

ERIK looks around at him.

> > ERIK
> > We're *all* seeing stars.

> > HARALD
> > No! I was hit on the head.

HARALD shakes his head as if to clear it.

80 EXT.   PLAIN OF ASGAARD   NIGHT

The longship falls and falls through the starry night
sky of space until it softly lands in a wide
wilderness.

81 EXT.   GOLDEN DRAGON IN THE PLAIN OF ASGAARD   NIGHT

On the deck the VIKINGS are huddled up, covered with
rime-frost.

MAGIC MUSIC

CLOSE-UP of ERIK. His face and brow are hung with ice.
With difficulty he opens his eyes. It seems as if he
has been lying there half-frozen for some time.
Perhaps the entire adventure has all been a dream, and
they have been stuck in the Arctic pack ice the whole
time. The hallucinations of men near to death.

ERIK looks around at the other huddled forms.

AUD is close to him.

He tries to speak, but his lips stick together. He
slumps back and shuts his eyes.

                    AUD
          Don't sleep ... wake ... Look!

Suddenly colored lights begin to play on his face.

ERIK opens his eyes again and looks in wonder.

                    ERIK
          Bi-Frost ... the Rainbow Bridge.

                                        CUT TO:

ERIK's POINT OF VIEW. There is the Aurora Borealis
stretched up, magnificent and awesome in the sky above
them.   .

                    ERIK
          Wake up!

The OTHERS slowly begin to rouse themselves from their
icy slumber and sit up, awed by the sight.

                    KEITEL
                 (whispering)
          Are we dead?

                    ERIK
                 (in an awed voice)
          The Rainbow Bridge.

                                   (CONTINUED)

                         VIKINGS
          Bi-Frost ...

They all peer up at the ever-changing colors of the
Aurora Borealis, hanging in the sky above them like
organ-pipes.

But something is happening. The lights begin to fade
to reveal a magical city on a mountain.

The MUSIC tells us that this is journey's end ... they
have reached Asgaard ... the City of the Gods.

The VIKINGS all catch their breaths and gaze in awe.

                         AUD
          Asgaard!

                         HARALD THE MISSIONARY
          Where?

                         SVEN's DAD
          Up there, you fathead.

                         HARALD THE MISSIONARY
          Up *where*?

HARALD looks around quizzically at the OTHERS. It is
clear that he can see nothing.

                         ERIK
          Look! It's real.

HARALD looks around at the OTHERS.

                         HARALD
          Hallucinations are real.

It's no use, HARALD can see nothing.

The VIKINGS, transfixed by the sight of their fabled
home of the Gods, rise to their feet.

MAGIC MUSIC fills the air.

AUD is standing beside ERIK. She whispers in his ear.

                         AUD
          The second note ...

                                        (CONTINUED)

                              ERIK
              The second note to wake the Gods ...

ERIK goes to the Horn Resounding. It is all covered
with ice.

                              AUD
                   Gently ...

ERIK blows ... a soft gentle note ... he takes his
mouth away and smiles at AUD. Once again the Horn
starts to vibrate and the note gets louder ... the
ship starts to vibrate ... once again it begins to
fill the stereo surround in the cinema ... louder and
louder ...

The whole landscape starts to vibrate ... louder and
louder grows the note until even the stars in the sky
are vibrating and then a magical thing starts to
happen ... The note fades as one by one the shimmering
stars start to fall out of the night sky ... they fall
like silver snow ... until the ship ... the VIKINGS
... Asgaard ... the whole landscape is covered with
sparkling dust ... then in the ensuing silence the
first light begins to glow in the Halls of Asgaard ...
then another ... and another ...

ERIK stares as if bewitched and slowly begins to climb
out of Golden Dragon ... but AUD tries to pull him
back.

                              AUD
                   Erik! You've done what you came to
                   do!

                              ERIK
                   Not quite ...

AUD looks at him.

                              AUD
                   Blow the third note! The note to take
                   us home!

                              ERIK
                   There is something I must ask the
                   Gods ...

                                        (CONTINUED)

                              AUD
               No living man has set foot in the
               Halls of Asgaard ... the Gods will
               never let you return.

ERIK looks at her ... for a moment ... but he knows he
has no choice.

                            SVEN
             I came to find my grandfather.

                            ERIK
             I have to go ...

                            AUD
             Then I shall come, too.

                            ERIK
                   (stares at her)
             No ... no ...

AUD embraces ERIK. ERIK breaks away.

                            ERIK
             But, Aud ... I ... I have come to
             find someone ...

AUD is about to say "Her?", but she bites the word
back and looks down at the ground.

                            ERIK
             I'm sorry, Aud ... I really am.

ERIK kisses her and then turns and climbs out of
Golden Dragon and sets off across the ice.

SVEN follows.

                          SVEN'S DAD
             Wait for me! I'll be dead soon
             anyway ...

                          KEITEL
             You can't go without me!

They follow.

HARALD looks mystified. He turns to AUD.

                                              (CONTINUED)

81 CONTINUED:

> HARALD
> Where do they think they're going?

AUD jerks herself out of the self-pity that was about
to descend upon her and turns to HARALD and smiles at
his disbelief.

> AUD
> Aren't you afraid?

> HARALD
> There's nothing for *me* to be afraid
> *of*.

AUD smiles and takes HARALD's hand and leads him after
the OTHERS.

The stars have fallen to form a shining, winding
pathway uo to the City of the Gods. This is what the
VIKINGS head for.

82 **EXT.   THE SKELETONS OF THE GIANTS   NIGHT**

Between them and the Citadel strange huge FORMS rise
up. The VIKINGS look at each other, wondering what
they are.

                                                    CUT TO:

A very WIDE SHOT to reveal the vast SKELETONS of the
GIANTS. The VIKINGS are but tiny gnat-sized figures
wending their way between the vast figures.

83 **EXT.   STAR PATH TO ASGAARD   NIGHT**

The VIKINGS climb the stairway-path of stars, up the
winding road to the massive Doors of Asgaard.

84 **EXT.   THE DOORS OF ASGAARD   NIGHT**

Once again the VIKINGS are tiny figures in a vast
landscape.

> ERIK
> Valhalla ...

HARALD THE MISSIONARY still can't see anything.

                                            (CONTINUED)

                          SVEN
                       (to HARALD)
               There! It's real! It's solid! Now do
               you believe us?

He pats the wall of Valhalla - the Great Hall. HARALD
reaches out, but his hand goes right through the wall.

                          HARALD
               There isn't anything.

HARALD THE MISSIONARY walks straight ahead through the
wall and disappears from sight.

The VIKINGS gasp.

HARALD reappears again.

                          HARALD
               You *are* having me on, aren't you?

                          ERIK
               It's Valhalla - where the warriors
               slain in battle go.

                          AUD
               It doesn't exist for him.

                          SVEN's DAD
               He's just a cynic.

ERIK can't reach the great handle ... he tries jumping
up to it but it's no good ...

ERIK bangs on the great doors. The OTHER VIKINGS join
in making a great din. Then they stop and every blow
echoes through the Halls of Asgaard and eventually
fades out across the wide wilderness around them.

                          ERIK
               Hallo! Let us in! We are the first
               living men to come to the Halls of
               Valhalla!

Then suddenly the door disintegrates and the VIKINGS
are buried under a pile of dust, from which they have
to extract themselves.

                          134

85 INT.   THE VESTIBULE OF VALHALLA   NIGHT

They find themselves in a vast, vaulted hall but to
their surprise it is derelict. The wind howls through
the empty windows and stalactites hang down from the
roof. The floor is a virgin carpet of untrodden snow
... snow that has collected in drifts against the
bases of pillars and in corners of the hall, covering
fallen masonry and broken objects alike.

HAUNTING MUSIC fills the air. Who will be the first to
leave his footprints in the Halls of the Gods?

ERIK slowly starts to cross the vast floor looking
around him as he does so. The dry snow squeaks under
the imprint of his feet ... one by one the other
VIKINGS follow.

                    ERIK
          Listen!

The VIKINGS listen. They hear the sound of children
laughing and shouting.

ERIK and his MEN walk through the columns toward a
pool of light. The scene that greets their eyes is not
at all what they had been prepared for.

86 INT.   VALHALLA   THE GREAT HALL   NIGHT

The Hall - Valhalla - is full of CHILDREN romping,
laughing, shouting, quarreling and playing games ...
chess, fencing, dice, tag, etc. around a wide hearth
fire.

WOMEN are cooking and doing other housewifely things
... weaving, making bread, etc. It is a thoroughly
domestic scene.

Suddenly one of them turns and looks at ERIK. It is
HELGA, whom ERIK accidentally killed in Scene One. She
is once again kneading dough. She has a red stain
under her breast.

                    HELGA
          Oh, good! It's Mr. Wonderful!

ERIK leaps to her side.

                                        (CONTINUED)

135

                              ERIK
              I've come to take you back to the
              land of the living.

                              HELGA
              What a stupid idea.

                              ERIK
                      (mortally hurt)
              Why?

                              HELGA
              What's the point of being dead in the
              land of the living?

                              ERIK
              I'll ask the Gods to give you life
              again!

HELGA looks at ERIK very skeptically. She obviously
doesn't think he knows what he's talking about. AUD
reacts. ERIK takes HELGA's hand - and gets covered
with dough.

                              HELGA
              Have you tried asking the Gods for
              anything?

                              ERIK
              Well ... no ...

                              HARALD THE MISSIONARY
              Who is he talking to?

                              AUD
              Sh!

                              HELGA
              Odin!

ONE OF THE CHILDREN throwing pennies against the wall,
looks around.

                              CHILD-ODIN
              I'm busy.

The VIKINGS are recovering from their surprise.

                              VIKINGS
              Odin?

                                           (CONTINUED)

                                    HELGA
                            (getting back to her
                            kneading)
                He's busy.

                                    ERIK
                Is *that* Odin?

                                    HELGA
                You'll have to wait until he's
                finished his game.

                                    ERIK
                            (shouts across)
                Odin!

HARALD is mystified. He looks around at the other
VIKINGS who are gazing earnestly at ODIN.

                                    HARALD
                You're *all* hallucinating!

                                    ERIK
                Odin!

ODIN looks up.

                                    ERIK
                We have come from the world of
                Midgard ...

The CHILD whom ODIN is playing with points his hand at
the ground near ERIK and a lightning bolt zaps into
it, sending the VIKINGS reeling back.

                                    CHILD-THOR
                Clear off.

                                    ODIN
                No, wait, Thor.

The CHILD-ODIN rises to his feet and approaches the
VIKINGS (who look very uncomfortable because this
isn't at all what they were expecting).

                                    ERIK
                You must help us.

                                    ODIN
                We don't *have* to help anybody.

                                              (CONTINUED)

                            137

                    ERIK
      Fenrir the Wolf covers the Sun - men
      fight and kill each other the whole
      time.

                    THOR
      Sounds great.

                    ODIN
      Why should *we* care?

                    ERIK
      Because ... you're ... you're the
      Gods ...

                    ODIN
      So?

                    ERIK
      Bring the Age of Ragnarok to an end
      and stop all this fighting and
      bloodshed.

HARALD looks around at the VIKINGS in increasing
desperation.

                    HARALD
      This is ridiculous.

                    VIKINGS
      Ssh!

                    HARALD
      Right!

The other CHILDREN-GODS have stopped playing around
now and are watching ERIK and ODIN.

                    ODIN
      Erik the Viking! The things you seek
      are not in our power.

                    ERIK
      But you're the Gods!

At this ODIN turns to the OTHER CHILDREN and smiles
ironically. The OTHER CHILDREN giggle.

                    ODIN
      Look ... Erik ...

                              (CONTINUED)

ODIN whistles. The OTHER CHILDREN look over their shoulders.

From out of the darkness of the perimeter of the Hall, shadows emerge ... shadows that, as they shuffle and stumble into the light, reveal themselves to be the HEROES that the VIKINGS had expected to find in Valhalla. But they are not hale and hearty giants quaffing mead and reliving their great battles ... they are, in fact, a sorry lot ... the Slain-in-Battle still bearing the hideous deformities of their fatal wounds. Most have a sword or axe buried in some part of their anatomy. One or two have been cleft in twain ...

The VIKINGS react to this grisly gathering as more and more of them emerge from the shadows.

They gasp as they notice SNORRI, IVAR, THORFINN, LOKI and LEIF THE LUCKY.

> ERIK
> Snorri! Ivar!

> HARALD
> Here we are on a bare mountaintop
> talking to thin air.

We notice that HARALD's cloak is being blown about as if he were indeed on a bare mountaintop. The OTHERS' cloaks are still.

SVEN'S DAD is gazing across at one HORRIBLY MUTILATED SPECIMEN.

> SVEN'S DAD
> Dad!

> KEITEL
> (disbelievingly)
> How can you tell?

> SVEN'S DAD
> I'll never forget him! the BASTARD!

SVEN reacts.

SVEN'S DAD starts to go berserk.

> SVEN'S DAD
> He drove me mad!

(CONTINUED)

139

                              SVEN
                  Easy, Dad!

                           SVEN's DAD
                  All his "you'll never be a Berserk if
                  you lose your temper" ...

                              SVEN
                  Dad!

                           SVEN'S DAD
                  I hate you! I hate you!

SVEN'S DAD collapses against SVEN and SVEN comforts
him, understandingly.

A FIGURE emerges from the throng of DEAD. It is
THORFINN. SVEN looks up at him.

                           THORFINN
                  You won, Sven.

                              ODIN
                  We do not make men love each other or
                  hate each other. Ask him!

ODIN points at one of the slain warriors. It is LOKI.

                              LOKI
                  What right have *you* to try and stop
                  men fighting, Erik the Viking? There
                  is glory in battle. There are riches
                  to be made and won ...

                           KEITEL
                  Made by *you*, Loki!

                              LOKI
                  By *you*, Keitel Blacksmith! Don't you
                  know, Erik, that is why he went with
                  you? Ragnarok was good for his
                  business ...

                           KEITEL
                  It's not my business any more!

Suddenly there is a howl ... a long ... a bitter howl
that echoes above and around the Halls of Asgaard and
that gets more distant and more distant. Everyone
(including the DEAD HEROES and the GODS) freezes and

                                        (CONTINUED)

looks up, listening. Perhaps we CUT AWAY to the
boiling sky as it resolves itself into the shape of a
WOLF that snarls and slinks away ...

ODIN turns to ERIK as the howling recedes.

>   ODIN
> Fenrir the Wolf has gone, Erik. But
> will men cease fighting each other?
> *That* is not in our power.

ODIN starts to laugh. All the OTHER CHILDREN start to
laugh ... so do the DEAD HEROES. ERIK and his MEN look
around uneasily.

>   ERIK
> I have one more request before we
> return ...

ERIK turns toward HELGA who is standing at her trough
of dough with her arms up to her elbows in flour. AUD
watches ERIK with sadness in her heart.

>   ODIN
> Return? You have set your foot in the
> Halls of Asgaard, Erik. You cannot
> return.

AUD looks around to see how the OTHERS react. It is as
she had feared. ERIK pales. The blood drains from the
OTHERS' faces.

AUD whispers something to HARALD. HARALD looks at her
blankly.

>   AUD
>   (whispering)
> *Please!*

>   HARALD
> But you're all imagining this ...
> whatever it is.

>   AUD
>   (earnestly)
> You're the only one who can. *Please!*

HARALD looks around at the dumb-founded VIKINGS. Then
he shrugs and wanders off, disappearing through the
closed doors of Valhalla.

(CONTINUED)

                          ERIK
              You mean ... we must stay here
              forever?

As he says this ERIK's eyes turn again toward HELGA.
He is clearly thinking at least there are
compensations ...

ODIN, however, is laughing again.

                          ODIN
              Stay *here*? Ha ha! This is Valhalla.
              This is reserved for those slain in
              battle.

                     HORRIBLY SLAIN WARRIOR
                        (grinning
                        cheerfully)
              Yeah! We're the *lucky* ones!

The Ghastly and Dismembered DEAD WARRIORS all chortle
to no end at the dismay written on the faces of ERIK
and his MEN.

At the same time there is a grinding, winching sound.
All those around the hearth-place fall back as a vast
grating is winched up from out of the flames.

The VIKINGS look at each other.

                          ODIN
              For *you* there is only the Pit of Hel!

As ODIN says this there is a roaring sound and the
flames and smoke are suddenly reversed and as the
roaring increases the flames are sucked down
altogether to reveal the black Pit of Hel itself. And
now the Pit is sucking the VIKINGS into it ... their
hair blows ... they try to withstand the force that is
drawing them toward the abyss ...

The GODS look on with some amusement. But some of the
DEAD are concerned.

                     SVEN'S GRANDFATHER
              Son! My son!

                     SVEN'S DAD
              Get lost!

                                        (CONTINUED)

                          142

                              SVEN
                    Dad! Grandfather!

                              VIKINGS
                    Help!

                              ERIK
                         (to Helga)
                    I tried to save you!

                              HELGA
                    Why should you care?

                              ERIK
                    I don't know! I just did!

But ERIK cannot withstand the force that is sucking
him down to the Pit of Hel.

He struggles to get a grip on the floor, but his hands
are all covered with dough.

Suddenly, however, SNORRI leaps from the ranks of the
DEAD. He grabs ERIK and tries to stop him from sliding
toward the Pit of Hel. But it's no good.

                              ERIK
                    No! Let go, Snorri!

                              SNORRI
                    I've got you!

                              ERIK
                    You'll be sucked down, too!

                              SNORRI
                    No! Arrgh!

Meanwhile, IVAR and THORFINN and LEIF THE LUCKY have
also leapt forward to save their COMRADES.

They put up a fantastic struggle but remorselessly
they are all sucked down.

Aagh!

The VIKINGS clutch at the stone floor, their fingers
trace blood as they try to cling on ... but to no
avail. The first are already toppling into the Pit.

                                        (CONTINUED)
                         143

                                    VIKINGS
                        Noooh!

                                    VIKINGS
                        Ah!

And the rest - including AUD - soon follow.

87 INT.   THE PIT OF HEL   NIGHT

     Inside the Pit of Hel, looking up. The mouth of the
     Pit of Hel, through which the VIKINGS are now tumbling
     higgledy-piggledy, is a round white disc set in the
     unutterable blackness of the pit. However, as the
     VIKINGS free-fall slowly toward CAMERA, they are lit
     up by a faint reddish glow from below. They are
     staring, wild-eyed and screaming as they fall.

     As they fall, KEITEL manages to smash his axe into the
     side of the pit. THORFINN grabs his leg and holds on
     to SVEN. LEIF clutches at SVEN's belt. SVEN'S DAD
     hangs on to SVEN's foot. IVAR clutches at THORFINN's
     foot. ERIK clutches IVAR's leg and AUD clutches
     ERIK's.

     They dangle like this for some seconds, and look
     fearfully beneath them.

88 INT.   HEL ITSELF   NIGHT

     As ERIK dangles we CUT TO the VIKINGS' eye-line to see
     down into the Pit of Hel ourselves - the Infernal
     Regions of flame and molten lava ... somehow suggests
     the face of a huge and sinister creature. No wonder
     they're scared out of their wits.

89 INT   THE PIT OF HEL   NIGHT

     ANGLE ON the dangling VIKINGS.

     ODIN and THOR appear at the top of the pit and look
     down with mild amusement. THOR casually points his
     hammer and a streak of lightning zaps KEITEL's axe. It
     instantly glows red-hot. KEITEL screams and has to let
     go.

     The OTHERS scream as they start to fall again.

                                              (CONTINUED)

89 CONTINUED:

We go to CLOSE-UPS of them falling and suddenly we hear a new sound - a long, high, sweet note.

CLOSE-UP of ERIK as he falls past CAMERA:

> ERIK
> Listen! LISTEN!

> AUD
> The third note!

90 EXT.   GOLDEN DRAGON IN THE PLAIN OF ASGAARD   NIGHT

HARALD THE MISSIONARY is blowing the Horn Resounding.

> HARALD THE MISSIONARY
> (to himself)
> I want to go home ... oooh!

Suddenly Golden Dragon, the Horn Resounding, and HARALD THE MISSIONARY shoot up into the air and disappear from sight.

91 INT.   THE PIT OF HEL   NIGHT

We are shooting from even further down the Pit, and the mouth is a smallish disc above them. The VIKINGS are looking down past CAMERA as they fall - they are still scared but gradually they start laughing ... laughing as they fall down and down until they fall past CAMERA and out of sight.

We are left with blackness and just the white disc of the mouth of the Pit of Hel above, and the Horn Resounding still sounds growing louder and louder - and the disc changes magically into the moon.

There is a series of OFF SCREEN splashes.

92 EXT.   RAVENSFJORD   DAWN

The note begins to fade and the CAMERA slowly PANS DOWN to reveal the VIKINGS all fallen into the duck pond back at Ravensfjord. They are laughing and whooping and splashing each other.

(CONTINUED)

145

                              ERIK
               I don't believe it ... ha ha ha! It
               brought us *home*!

                              LEIF
               But who *blew* it?

                              SVEN
                         (looking around)
               Must have been Harald.

                              SNORRI
               Well, where's *he* then?

                              IVAR
               Oh! Who cares? We're *home*!

                              THORFINN
               Mum! Dad!

                              SVEN
               We're back!

SVEN embraces his FATHER and dances him around with
joy.

                              ALL
               Yoo-hoo! We're here! We're ...

Suddenly the joy drains from their faces and they gape
in horror. The CAMERA remains on their individual
faces for some moments. What is it that they see?

Eventually we CUT to see that out of the huts the
WOMEN and CHILDREN and OLD MEN are emerging - but they
are anything but happy. In fact they are all bound and
gagged.

Behind them emerge the sinister figures of HALFDAN THE
BLACK, GISLI and EILIF and maybe half a dozen ARMED
MEN.

HALFDAN and his CRONIES no longer look sleek and
self-assured. They are haggard and desperate. Their
faces are streaked with dirt and sweat, and their
clothes are torn and soiled. They have clearly been
going through a lean time since Ragnarok ended, and
they have descended on the village for revenge and for
whatever plunder they can find. They have a few
sackfuls of booty with them.

                                        (CONTINUED)

They herd the WOMEN, CHILDREN and OLD MEN into a
pathetic huddle in the middle of the village.

HALFDAN is spitting evil and hatred.

> HALFDAN
> You're just in time, Erik the Viking.

ERIK makes a move, but HALFDAN nods at the WOMEN and
CHILDREN.

> HALFDAN
> Throw down your weapons - or we shoot
> the children first.

ERIK hesitates ... the OTHERS look at him. What choice
have they? Reluctantly, ERIK throws his weapons onto
the dry land. The OTHERS follow suit.

HALFDAN watches. His MEN stand around him in a tight
group with their backs to each other.

> HALFDAN
> Good ... good ... right, now we'll
> just shoot everybody at once ...

ERIK is paralyzed. What can they do? Half HALFDAN's
MEN are aiming their crossbows at ERIK and his
COMRADES, and half are aiming at the WOMEN and
CHILDREN.

They raise their crossbows to shoot. Their fingers
tighten on the triggers.

Suddenly there is a scream from above. EVERYONE looks
up and, amazingly, out of the sky falls GOLDEN DRAGON
and lands fair and square on top of HALFDAN and his
GANG, squashing them flat.

HARALD THE MISSIONARY staggers blearily from the
wreckage.

GRIMHILD HOUSEWIFE has got her gag off.

> GRIMHILD
> Harald!

She rushes to HARALD, while the VIKINGS rush to
release their LOVED ONES.

(CONTINUED)

ERIK checks to see that HALFDAN is really dead. He is
- as a Dodo.

> IVAR
>> Look!

They all turn and see the Sun rising.

The VILLAGERS gasp in wonder. They've never seen the
Sun before.

> ERIK
>> Now it's up to us.

He looks around and sees THORFINN and SVEN with their
arms around each other. ERIK grins.

AUD catches his eye and sadly she averts her gaze.

> ERIK
>> The Gods cannot make us love each
>> other - we must find that for
>> ourselves ... each and every one of
>> us.

AUD looks up as ERIK smiles at her and then takes her
hand.

Then they ALL turn and gaze at the spectacle of the
Sun returning to the World.

THE END

A JOHN GOLDSTONE/PROMINENT FEATURES PRODUCTION

ERIK THE VIKING

TIM ROBBINS
GARY CADY
TERRY JONES
EARTHA KITT
MICKEY ROONEY
JOHN CLEESE
TSUTOMU SEKINE
ANTONY SHER
JOHN GORDON SINCLAIR
IMOGEN STUBBS
SAMANTHA BOND
FREDDIE JONES
TIM McINNERNY
CHARLES McKEOWN
RICHARD RIDINGS
DANNY SCHILLER
Casting IRENE LAMB
Make-Up & Hair Designer JENNY SHIRCORE
Costume Designer PAM TAIT
Conceptual Designer ALAN LEE
Special Effects Designer RICHARD CONWAY
Second Unit Director JULIAN DOYLE
Music NEIL INNES
Film Editor GEORGE AKERS
Production Designer JOHN BEARD
Photographed by IAN WILSON
Association Producer NEVILLE C. THOMPSON
Executive Producer TERRY GLINWOOD
Produced by JOHN GOLDSTONE
Written & Directed by TERRY JONES

CREDITS

Erik .... TIM ROBBINS
Erik's Grandfather .... MICKEY ROONEY
Freya .... EARTHA KITT
King Arnulf .... TERRY JONES
Aud .... IMOGEN STUBBS
Halfdan the Black .... JOHN CLEESE
Slavemaster .... TSUTOMU SEKINE
Loki .... ANTONY SHER
Keitel Blacksmith .... GARY CADY
Sven's Dad .... CHARLES McKEOWN
Sven the Berserk .... TIM McINNERNY
Ivar the Boneless .... JOHN GORDON SINCLAIR
Thorfinn Skull-Splitter .... RICHARD RIDINGS
Helga .... SAMANTHA BOND
Harald the Missionary .... FREDDIE JONES
Snorri the Miserable .... DANNY SCHILLER
Ernest the Viking (a Rapist) .... JIM BROADBENT
Jennifer the Viking (another Rapist) .... JIM CARTER
Erik's Mum .... MATYELOK GIBBS
Unn-the-Thrown-at .... TILLY VOSBURGH
Leif the Lucky .... JAY SIMPSON
Ingemund the Old .... JOHN SCOTT MARTIN
Thorhild the Sarcastic .... SIAN THOMAS
Grimhild Housewife .... SARAH CROWDEN
Mordfiddle the Cook .... BERNARD PADDEN
Ulf the Unmemorable .... BERNARD LATHAM
Thorfinn's Mum .... JULIA McCARTHY
Thorfinn's Dad .... ALLAN SURTEES
Ivar's Mum .... SANDRA VOE
Thorkatla the Indiscreet .... ANGELA CONNOLLY
Leif's Pregnant Girlfriend .... SALLY JONES
Ornulf/Chamberlain/Dog Soldier .... ANDREW MACLACHLAN
Bjarni/Halfdan's Guard/Musician .... TIM KILLICK
Thangbrand/Citizen/Dog Soldier .... GRAHAM McTAVISH
Gisli the Chiseller .... CYRIL SHAPS
Eilif the Mongol Horde/Musician .... PETER GEEVES
Prisoner .... PADDY JOYCE
Prisoner .... COLIN HARPER
Prisoner .... HARRY JONES
Prisoner .... BARRY McCARTHY

Prisoner	GARY ROOST
Hy Brasilian	NEIL INNES
Odin	SIMON EVANS
Thor	MATTHEW BAKER
Horribly Slain Warrior	DAVE DUFFY
Even More Horribly Slain Warrior	FRANK BEDNASH

This film is *not* based on the children's book *The Saga of Erik the Viking* by Terry Jones (although he hopes it will help the sales).

Production Manager	CHRIS THOMPSON
First Assistant Director	DAVID BROWN
Second Assistant Director	GERRY TOOMEY
Production Manager—Norway	INGE TENVIK
Third Assistant Director	NEIL CALDER
Location Manager—Malta	MIKE HIGGINS
Assistant Production Manager—Norway	KNUT ERIK JENSEN
Production Co-ordinator	JOYCE TURNER
Assistant to producer	LISA BONNICHON
Production Co-ordinator—Malta	RITA GALEA
Tromso Facilities	LOKOMOTIV
Second Unit Assistant Director	MARGARITA DOYLE
Casting (U.S.A.)	JOHN LYONS
	DONNA ISAACSON
Script Supervisor	LIBBIE BARR
Production Accountant	ANDY BIRMINGHAM
Accounts Assistants	YVONE EASTMOND
	LESLEY BRODERICK
	JEAN SIMMONS
Camera Operator	IAN WILSON
Focus	KENNY BYRNE
Clapper Loader	SIMON RICHARDS
Grip	MALCOLM HUSE
Second Unit Operator	LUKE CARDIFF
Second Unit Camera Assistant	MARK STRASBURG
Second Unit Grip	TONY ANDREWS
Camera Trainee	JULIA DALY
Special Effects Editor	DENNIS McTAGGART
Sound Editor	ALAN BELL
Dialogue Editors	MICHAEL HOPKINS
	BRIAN TILLING

Footsteps Editor	TONY MESSAGE, GBFE
First Assistant Editor	JASON ADAMS
Assistant Editors	CHARLES IRELAND
	KEITH MASON
	GEOFF BROWN
Cutting Room Trainee	ANGIE WILLS
Optical Effects	PEERLESS CAMERA CO. LTD.
Optical Effects Supervisor	KENT HOUSTON
Co-ordinator	MARTIN BODY
Optical Cameramen	NICK DUNLOP
	TIM OLLIVE
	STEVE CUTMORE
	DOUG FORREST
	LES BROUGHTON
Rotoscoping	JANICE BODY
	RASHID KHARES
High-Speed Photography	PETER TYLER
	KENNETH GRAY
Matte Camera	JOHN GRANT
	ROY CARNELL
Matte Painters	DOUG FERRIS
	BOB CUFF
	JOY CUFF
Blue Screen Consultants	DENNIS BARTLETT & STAN SAYERS
Art Directors	GAVIN BOCQUET
	ROGER CAIN
Assistant Art Director	LUCY RICHARDSON
Art Department Assistant	JIM EVOY
Supervising Sculptor/Modeller	PETER VOYSEY
Set Decorator	JOAN WOOLLARD
Production Buyer	IAN GILADJIAN
Wardrobe Supervisor	PATRICK WHEATLEY
Wardrobe Assistants	RENEE HEIMER
	MARION WEISE
Assistant to Costume Designer	KARI FURRE
Make-Up Artists	SARAH GRUNDY
	AILEEN SEATON
	ANNIE McEWAN
	LINDA CROZIER
Sound Recordist	BOB DOYLE
Boom Operator	PAUL FILBY

Sound Maintenance	JASON RUSSELL
Dubbing Mixers	HUGH STRAIN
	BILL ROWE
A.D.R. Mixers	TED SWANSCOTT
	LIONEL STRUTT
Music Mixer	AUSTIN INCE
Orchestrator/Conductor	JOHN ALTMAN
Music Supervisor	RAY WILLIAMS
Special Effects Supervisor	PETER HUTCHINSON
Special Effects Senior Technicians	ROBERT HOLLOW
	MARTIN GANT
	STEPHEN HAMILTON
Special Effects Technicians	DAVID McCALL
	CHRISTINE OVERS
	DAVE ELTHAM
Special Effects Assistant	STEPHEN HUTCHINSON
Special Effects Modeller	RAY SCOTT
Special Effects Engineer	LESLIE WHEELER
Special Effects Buyer	KAYE MOSS
Sup. Special Effects Plasterer	ALLAN CROUCHER
Animatronics Designer	JAMIE COURTIER
Marine Consultant	DAVID RAINE
Gaffer	NORMAN SMITH
Chief Electrician	ALFIE EMMINS
Electricians	DAVE RIDOUT
	DEAN KENNEDY
	DAVE ESCOFFREY
	TERRY McGUINNESS
	FRED BRADLEY
	TOMMY CASEY
Property Master	BARRY WILKINSON
Standby Props	JOE DIPPLE
	GARY IXER
Property Men	KEITH PITT
	PHILIP KENNEDY
	CHARLES IXER
	REG WHEELER
	STEPHEN WILKINSON
Unit Publicist	SUSAN D'ARCY
Stills Photographer	DAVID APPLEBY
Publicity Secretary	REBECCA WEST

Publicity Consultants...CORBETT & KEENE
Stunt Co-ordinator .... MARTIN GRACE
Stunts...EDDIE POWELL
                                                BILL WESTON
Construction Manager..PETER VERARD
Construction Manager—Malta... ALVARO BELSOLE
Assistant Construction Manager—U.K.................................... CRAIG HILLER
Standby Stagehand... DAVID JONES
Standby Carpenter ....RICHARD JONES
Standby Plasterer...DAVID T. WICKS
Supervising Carpenter..LEON APSEY
H.O.D. Painter.. ALAN GRENHAM
Painter .... KENNETH WELLAND
H.O.D. Rigger .... HARRY HEEKS
Standby Rigger .... LES BEAVER
Supervising Stagehand ....CLIVE RIVERS
H.O.D. Plasterer...DAVID B. WICKS
Travel & Freight.. SULLIVAN TRAVELWIDE—Malta
                                    THOS. C. SMITH & CO.—Malta
                                        RENOWN FREIGHT—U.K.
                                        THE TRAVEL COMPANY
                            D&D LOCATION FACILITIES—U.K.
                                            FOCUS CARS
Unit Drivers... TERRY REECE
                                        BRIAN BROOKNER
                                      MAURICE NEWSON
                                          TONY TROMP
Prominent Features .... ANNE JAMES
                                        ALISON DAVIES
                                            IAN MILES
                                        LIZ LEHMANS
Malta Film Facilities ....PAUL AVELLINO
Post Production Facilities & Recording ...... DE LANE LEA SOUND CENTRE
Final Mix ....GOLDCREST ELSTREE STUDIOS
Music Recorded at... SNAKE RANCH
Additional A.D.R...................................... MAYFLOWER FILM RECORDING
Titles ....TREVOR BOND
Golden Dragon Constructed by ....SQUARE SAIL—Bristol
Old Norse Dialogue supplied by ....UNIVERSITY OF CAMBRIDGE
                                        DEPARTMENT OF ANGLO-
                                        SAXON, NORSE AND CELTIC

Dupes Supplied by .... FILM & PHOTO DESIGN
Lighting .... LEE ELECTRIC (LIGHTING) LIMITED
Film Originated on .... FUJICOLOR
Cameras by .... SAMUELSONS, LONDON
Grip Equipment by .... GRIP HOUSE, LONDON
Costumes from .... TWENTIETH CENTURY
                                                        COSTUMES, LONDON
Insurance by .... BAYLY, MARTIN & FAY
                                                        INTERNATIONAL
Completion Guarantee Supplied by .... THE COMPLETION BOND
                                                        COMPANY
Underwritten & Financed by .... GOTABANKEN, LONDON
                                                        BRANCH

Made at Mediterranean Film Studios, Malta; Lee International Studios, Shepperton, England; and on location in Tromso, Norway.

TECHNICOLOR ®

MPAA no. 29792

DOLBY STEREO